HEDGES
& BOUNDARIES

All you need to know about creating and
maintaining hedges, fences and walls

ALAN TOOGOOD

SELECT
EDITIONS

A SALAMANDER BOOK

©1986 Salamander Books Ltd.

This edition published 1991 by
Selectabook Ltd.,
Folly Road,
Roundway,
Devizes,
Wiltshire, U.K.
SN10 2HR.

ISBN 0 86101 217 8

Credits
Editor: John Woodward
Designer: Kathy Gummer
Copy editor: Edward Bunting
Filmset: Modern Text Ltd.

Colour reproductions:
Rodney Howe Ltd.
Printed in Belgium by
Proost International Book
Production, Turnhout

AUTHOR

Alan Toogood trained at the Royal Botanic Gardens at Kew, Surrey and the Parks and Gardens Department at Brighton, Sussex, before going on to a two-year studentship at the Royal Horticultural Society's garden at Wisley, Surrey. He worked as a horticultural journalist on *Gardeners' Chronicle* and *Amateur Gardening* magazines, and later became Lecturer in Horticulture and Nursery Practices at Merrist Wood Agricultural College. For several years he was Editor of the monthly magazine *Greenhouse*. He is now a freelance horticultural journalist and consultant, the author of many gardening books, and Horticulture Correspondent for *The Times*.

Consultant

Ann Bonar has been a horticultural writer and consultant for more than 20 years, and has written many books on various aspects of gardening. She is a regular contributor to a variety of gardening periodicals and trade journals, and has taken part in a number of gardening programmes broadcast by the BBC. For 12 years she has answered readers' queries sent in to a leading British weekly gardening magazine.

CONTENTS

INTRODUCTION

If you want to make your garden look attractive and professional you have to give careful thought to the boundaries. Hedging and fencing is a craft all of its own, but once you have defined your boundary, the choice of materials and design are all yours, and this can lead you to some highly creative and satisfying activity. Your garden cannot fail to be the better for it.

GARDEN BOUNDARIES

Traditionally gardens are enclosed in some way, whether for privacy or simply to mark the boundary, this normally being achieved with fences of various kinds, walls, hedges or other living screens.

However, a current trend, particularly on modern housing estates, is the open-plan front garden. Regulations may prevent you from putting up full-sized hedges, walls or fences. But even here you can still define the boundary attractively and effectively, ensuring at least that the garden is not used as public highway.

Hedges, fences, ornamental walls and so on can also be used

Below: *The boundary should suit the style of the house. This cottage has a low picket fence in traditional style.*

within the garden, perhaps to divide it and so create elements of surprise, or to screen utility areas such as the vegetable plot or the fruit garden.

MATERIALS AND DESIGN

In this book all kinds of plants suitable for hedges and screens are considered, including full details of how to plant and maintain them.

All the materials available for constructing walls, fences and

Below: *Dry-stone retaining walls make an attractive front boundary in a sloping garden and can be planted with rock plants.*

other artificial screens are looked at objectively, with guidance on constructing these features.

The book contains a wealth of ideas, such as screening for noise, sun, wind or privacy, but this is not just a collection of ideas: all the practical aspects have been thoroughly covered.

Apart from being of value to those who want to plant or construct new features, owners of established hedges, screens or so on will also find this book helpful for its advice and insight into the maintenance aspects.

The illustrations, many of which were specially commissioned, will, we hope, provide further inspiration.

FORMAL HEDGES

Hedges are very popular for marking the boundaries of a garden. They form pleasing natural backgrounds for other plants, provide wind protection and can create impenetrable barriers to keep out all intruders (particularly if prickly plants are chosen). Formal hedges need training and regular clipping, but are the first choice of most gardeners.

PLANTS USED

A formal hedge is one that is trained to a definite shape. This shape is maintained by regular clipping or trimming, either once or several times per year according to speed of growth.

Three basic types of plants are used: shrubs, trees and conifers. They may be deciduous (drop their leaves in the autumn), such as beech and hornbeam, or evergreen (hold on to their leaves all the year round), like yew, Lawson cypress, holly and laurel.

Evergreen hedges, of course, give all year round privacy and are particularly recommended for windy, exposed or seaside gardens. It is useful to know that beech and hornbeam, when grown as hedging, actually hang on to their dead leaves throughout the winter, shedding them just before the new foliage is produced in the spring. Thus they are a lovely golden-brown colour all through winter.

USES

Formal hedges are ideal for garden boundaries as they are fairly narrow and do not spread much, so there is little risk of the hedge spreading onto public footpaths or neighbours' gardens (provided, of course, they are clipped regularly). However, it should be said that over the years they may gradually get wider, and taller, particularly if they are clipped only lightly. Ideally one should not allow this to happen, but if it does,

Below: *Yew,* Taxus baccata, *makes a really dense hedge and is not as slow growing as many people imagine. Needs regular clipping.*

remember that most subjects can be cut back fairly hard.

Formal hedges can also be used within the garden to divide it or to screen objects or utility areas. For example, the vegetable plot could be separated from the ornamental part with a formal hedge.

SHAPE

It is best to train the hedge to a wedge shape: that is, wider at the base than at the top, with the sides gradually sloping inwards from bottom to top. The top should generally be about half the width of the bottom. This ensures maximum light reaches the sides of the hedge, which results in better growth and leaf production. This shape also sheds snow more easily: if snow is allowed to build up on top of a hedge the weight can split it, and the shape may then be lost

Below: *Formal hedge shapes. (1) and (2) are typical wedge shapes, (3) is a serpentine hedge, and (4) has a castellated top.*

forever. A wedge shape also gives a stronger, denser hedge.

You have a choice between a flat or a rounded top for your formal hedge, and some gardeners prefer more intricate shapes, such as a castellated top. The hedge does not have to follow a straight line either; you can train it to a wavy shape, and this is known as a serpentine hedge. Intricate shapes like this, of course, are more time consuming to train and trim.

SIZES

For ease of clipping, and to prevent too much shade, do not be tempted to allow a formal hedge to get too high. Many people keep a hedge at around 5ft (1·5m) in height, but for more privacy it could go to 6ft (1·8m). If you can manage to clip it, a formal hedge can be allowed to grow to a maximum height of 8ft (2·4m).

Formal hedges should ideally be about 3-4ft (1-1·2m) wide at the base, tapering to about half this at the top.

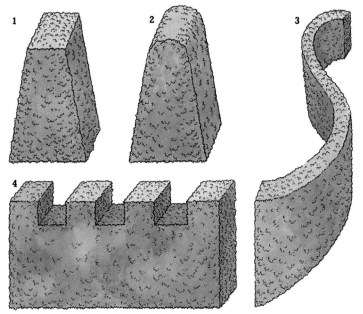

PLANTS FOR FORMAL HEDGES

There are many shrubs and trees which are suitable for training into formal hedges. A very comprehensive range is given here.

As well as descriptions of the plants, and their special uses and requirements, the table gives planting distances and times for pruning or trimming. Unless otherwise stated, all these plants are capable of forming hedges of 6ft (1·8m) plus. The exceptions are the plants suitable for dwarf or low-growing hedges.

Right: *Gold and green varieties of* Lawson cypress *are very attractive.*
Far right: Lonicera nitida *makes a dense formal hedge.*

Name	Foliage/habit
Berberis thunbergii Atropurpurea and 'Red Chief' (barberry)	Deciduous; small leaves, red-purple, spiny stems
Berberis thunbergii 'Atropurpurea Nana' (barberry)	Deciduous; small leaves, red-purple, spiny stems
Buxus sempervirens (box)	Evergreen; small leaves, deep green
Buxus sempervirens 'Suffruticosa (dwarf edging box)	Evergreen; small leaves, deep green and shiny
Carpinus betulus (hornbeam)	Deciduous; large oval green leaves which turn brown and are held throughout winter
Chamaecyparis lawsoniana 'Green Hedger' (Lawson cypress)	Evergreen; sprays of rich green
Corylus maxima 'Purpurea' (purple-leaf filbert)	Deciduous; large, rounded, deep purple leaves
Cotoneaster simonsii	Semi-evergreen; small, rounded, green leaves
Crataegus monogyna (hawthorn)	Deciduous; green, lobed leaves and spiny stems
X *Cupressocyparis leylandii* (Leyland cypress)	Evergreen; sprays of deep green foliage
Cupressus macrocarpa (Monterey cypress)	Evergreen; sprays of bright green foliage
Elaeagnus x *ebbingei*	Evergreen; large, oval leaves, silvery below
Euonymus japonicus	Evergreen; oval, glossy green leaves

Planting distance/clipping time	Special uses or conditions
18in (45cm) Midsummer and midwinter	A tough plant, ideal for clay or chalk soils.
12in (30cm) Midsummer and midwinter	Ditto; suitable for a dwarf hedge
18in (45cm); once a month late spring to late summer	Grows well in chalky soils
6in (15cm); once a month late spring to late summer	For a dwarf hedge; grows well on chalk
18in (45cm) Late summer	Good for exposed sites, chalk and clay soils
24in (60cm) Late summer	Good for exposed sites and heavy soils
18in (45cm) Spring or late summer	Excellent for exposed sites and chalk soil
18in (45cm) Late summer	Ideal for seaside gardens and chalk or clay soils
12in (30cm); once a month late spring to late summer	Good for seaside gardens, windy sites and clay soils
24in (60cm) Late summer	Good for exposed and seaside gardens, and chalky soils
24in (60cm) Spring and late summer	Recommended only for mild and seaside gardens
24in (60cm) Spring or late summer	Ideal for seaside and exposed gardens
18in (45cm) Spring or late summer	Tolerates seaside conditions, shade, sun and pollution

PLANTS FOR FORMAL HEDGES

Name	Foliage/habit
Fagus sylvatica (beech)	Deciduous; large, oval leaves which turn golden-brown and are held throughout winter
Griselinia littoralis	Evergreen, large, rounded, light green leaves, rather leathery
Ilex aquifolium and cultivars (holly)	Evergreen; large, deep green and very prickly leaves
Laurus nobilis (sweet bay)	Evergreen; large, deep green, shiny leaves
Lavandula angustifolia and cultivars (lavender)	Evergreen; long, narrow, grey-green leaves
Ligustrum ovalifolium (oval-leaf privet)	Evergreen; small, oval, green leaves
Ligustrum ovalifolium 'Aureum' (golden privet)	Evergreen; small, oval, bright yellow leaves
Lonicera nitida (Chinese honeysuckle)	Evergreen; very tiny, oval, green leaves
Prunus cerasifera (myrobalan)	Deciduous; large, oval, green leaves
Prunus cerasifera 'Nigra' (myrobalan)	Deciduous; large, oval, deep purple leaves
Prunus x cistena (purple-leaf sand cherry)	Deciduous; large, oval, deep red leaves
Prunus laurocerasus and var. 'Rotundifolia' (cherry laurel)	Evergreen; very large, ovate leaves, deep green and glossy
Prunus lusitanica (Portugal laurel)	Evergreen; large, ovate, deep green, glossy leaves
Prunus spinosa 'Purpurea' (blackthorn)	Deciduous; ovate, green leaves, very spiny stems
Pyracantha rogersiana (firethorn)	Evergreen; narrow, oval, green leaves, spiny stems
Rhododendron ponticum	Evergreen; large, lanceolate, deep green leaves
Taxus baccata (yew)	Evergreen; narrow, deep green leaves
Thuja occidentalis (white cedar)	Evergreen; flat sprays of deep green leaves
Thuja plicata 'Atrovirens' (western red cedar)	Evergreen; flat sprays of glossy, bright green foliage
Viburnum tinus (laurustinus)	Evergreen; large, ovate, deep green leaves

Planting distance/clipping time	Special uses or conditions
18in (45cm) Late summer	Ideal for chalky soils and windy areas
24in (60cm) Early summer	Recommended only for mild and coastal areas; good on chalk
18in (45cm) Late summer	Ideal for seaside gardens and heavy soil
18in (45cm) Late summer	Needs good drainage; suitable for seaside gardens
12in (30cm) Immediately after flowering	For dwarf hedges; needs good drainage; suitable for seaside gardens
12in (30cm) Mid-spring to late summer as needed	Takes exposure, chalk and pollution
Ditto	Ditto
Ditto	Tolerates chalk and heavy soils
18in (45cm) Mid-spring and again in early summer	A tough plant which grows well on chalk
18in (45cm) Mid-spring or early summer	A tough plant which grows well on chalk
Ditto	Ditto. Forms a low hedge
24in (60cm) Summer	Best to avoid chalk soils and exposure
24in (60cm) Summer	Very hardy, ideal for exposed gardens, chalk and shade
12in (30cm) Spring or summer	A very tough plant, grows well on chalk
12in (30cm) Spring or early summer	A tough and adaptable shrub
24in (60cm) Early summer	Needs acid soil; tolerates windy sites
18in (45cm) Late summer	Tolerates a windy site, chalky and heavy soils, and shade
24in (60cm) Late summer	Adaptable, needs well-drained soil
24in (60cm) Late summer	Grows well in chalky and heavy soils
18in (45cm) Spring or summer	Ideal for seaside, windy and chalky gardens, and shade

15

INFORMAL HEDGES

Perhaps you have a country cottage or informal garden, and do not want the rigid lines of a formal hedge. In this instance allow the hedging plants to grow naturally, maybe choosing some that have eye-catching flowers or berries.

PLANTS USED

An informal hedge is one that is allowed to grow naturally, with little or no clipping, although some trimming may be necessary to reduce any over-long shoots.

Shrubs and trees are used, both evergreen and deciduous, especially those with attractive flowers, berries or leaves. Because the hedge is not trimmed (or not trimmed hard) the plants will flower each year, so you can if desired have a really colourful hedge. It is worth bearing in mind that some of the subjects recommended for informal hedges can also be used for formal hedges, but of course the clipping may prevent the flowers and berries developing.

Examples of plants often used for informal hedges include *Berberis darwinii* (barberry), a flowering evergreen; *Berberis × stenophylla* (barberry), also a flowering evergreen; *Cotoneaster simonsii*, an evergreen with attractive berries; *Escallonia rubra macrantha*, a flowering evergreen; *Elaeagnus pungens* 'Maculata', an evergreen with colourful foliage; and *Tamarix gallica* (tamarisk), a deciduous shrub with attractive flowers and foliage. Full details of these, and many others, will be found in the plant lists on pages 18-21.

USES

Informal hedges are not so suitable for boundaries around small gardens, as they can

Below: Forsythia x intermedia *'Spectabilis' is an excellent shrub for an informal hedge and flowers in spring. The less it is trimmed the more flowers it produces. It is deciduous so will look bare in the winter.*

Above left: Olearia x haastii *or daisy bush, as an informal hedge, flowering in summer.*
Above right: *A hedge of Leyland cypress, and in the foreground* Potentilla fruticosa *variety, which makes a low informal hedge.*

rapidly encroach onto public footpaths or neighbours' gardens —unless they are planted well back with sufficient space for full development. However, this takes up a great deal of ground. This wide-spreading habit is a disadvantage of the informal hedge. There is no problem, of course, if you have a large garden.

Space permitting, informal hedges can make attractive features within the garden, to divide it and to screen parts of it. They usually provide more colour and interest than most formal hedges.

It is also possible to compromise and have semi-formal hedges, by cutting back lightly, particularly at the sides. In this way, at least some flowers or berries are produced, without the hedge taking up too much ground.

SHAPES

A truly informal hedge is left to grow to its natural shape. Some plants, for instance, have a pleasing arching habit of growth, such as *Berberis* × *stenophylla*. Others form 'mounds' of growth, examples being *Escallonia rubra macrantha* and *Elaeagnus pungens* 'Maculata'.

SIZES

It is best to choose plants that do not grow too tall, otherwise they create too much shade. Of course, this may not be a problem in a large garden. It is suggested that plants which grow to around 6-8ft (1·8-2·4m) in height would be ideal. However, you can always give even the most informal of hedges the occasional pruning on top, so as to limit its height.

As for width, again the plants should ideally be left to grow to their full extent. Most of those recommended are very bushy and capable of spreading to at least 6-8ft (1·8-2·4m), so do take this into account when planning for an informal hedge.

PLANTS FOR INFORMAL HEDGES

Name	Foliage, flowers and berries
Arundinaria japonica (bamboo)	Evergreen; broad, grassy leaves
Atriplex halimus (tree purslane)	Semi-evergreen; silvery grey leaves
Berberis buxifolia 'Nana' (barberry)	Evergreen; yellow flowers in spring; prickly stems
B. darwinii (barberry)	Evergreen; deep yellow flowers in spring; bluish berries; prickly habit
B. x stenophylla (barberry)	Evergreen; golden-yellow flowers in spring; prickly habit
B. verruculosa (barberry)	Evergreen; golden-yellow flowers in spring; prickly habit
Camellia (any bushy-growing species)	Evergreen; red, pink or white flowers in winter/spring
Cotoneaster franchetii	Semi-evergreen; orange berries in autumn
C. lacteus	Evergreen; red berries in autumn and winter
C. simonsii	Semi-evergreen; large red berries in autumn
Elaeagnus pungens 'Maculata'	Evergreen; green leaves heavily splashed yellow
Escallonia rubra macrantha	Evergreen; rose-red flowers in summer
Forsythia x intermedia 'Spectabilis'	Deciduous; yellow flowers in spring
Fuchsia magellanica and *F.* 'Riccartonii'	Deciduous; scarlet and violet flowers in summer
Hebe x andersonii (shrubby veronica)	Evergreen; mauve flowers in summer and autumn
Hebe rakaiensis (shrubby veronica)	Evergreen; white flowers in summer
Hibiscus syriacus	Deciduous; blue, red, pink or white flowers in summer and autumn
Hippophae rhamnoides (sea buckthorn)	Deciduous; silvery leaves; orange berries in autumn and winter
Hydrangea macrophylla (hortensia varieties)	Deciduous; flowers in shades of red, pink, blue and white in summer
Lavandula angustifolia and varieties (lavender)	Evergreen; lavender-blue flowers in summer
Olearia avicennifolia (daisy bush)	Evergreen; white flowers in summer

Planting distance and pruning time	Special uses or conditions
24in (60cm) No pruning needed	Ideal for windy gardens and moist soils
18in (45cm) Spring	Ideal for seaside gardens; takes salty soils
12in (30cm) Early summer	Dwarf hedge; slow grower; ideal for chalk soils
18in (45cm) Early summer	Grows well in chalky soils
18in (45cm) Early summer	Ditto
12in (30cm) Early summer	Slow grower; does well on chalk
24in (60cm) Immediately after flowering	Must have acid soil
18in (45cm) Late summer	Very adaptable: can be grown by the sea, on chalk and in clay
18in (45cm) Late summer	Ditto
24in (60cm) Late summer	Ditto
24in (60cm) Spring or late summer	Especially good for seaside gardens
24in (60cm) Summer, after flowering	Especially good for seaside gardens and chalky soils
18in (45cm) Spring, after flowering	Very hardy and adaptable
12in (30cm) Early-mid spring	Ideal for seaside gardens
12in (30cm) Spring	Dwarf hedge; ideal for seaside gardens
12in (30cm) Spring	
18-24in (45-60cm) Spring, but rarely necessary	Plenty of sun needed
24in (60cm) Summer	Ideal for seaside gardens; tolerates exposure
24in (60cm) Spring	Ideal for seaside; needs moist soil. Fairly low hedge
12in (30cm) Autumn	Dwarf hedges; good for seaside gardens
18in (45cm) Late spring	Suitable for seaside gardens and chalky soils. but needs shelter

PLANTS FOR INFORMAL HEDGES

Name	Foliage, flowers and berries
O. x haastii (daisy bush)	Evergreen; white flowers in summer
O. macrodonta (daisy bush)	Evergreen; holly-like leaves; white flowers in early summer
Philadelphus microphyllus (mock orange blossom)	Deciduopus, fragrant white flowers, early summer
Poncirus trifoliata (Japanese bitter orange)	Deciduous; very spiny stems; scented white flowers in spring
Potentilla fruticosa 'Katherine Dykes' (shrubby cinquefoil)	Deciduous; large yellow flowers in summer and autumn
Pyracantha atalantioides and *P. x watereri* (firethorns)	Evergreen; red berries in autumn
Rhododendron luteum (yellow azalea)	Deciduous; scented yellow flowers in late spring
R. ponticum	Evergreen; mauve flowers in early summer
Ribes sanguineum (flowering currant)	Deciduous; red or pink flowers in spring
Rosa, hybrid musk roses 'Cornelia', 'Felicia' and 'Penelope'	Deciduous; scented pink flowers, summer to autumn
R. rugosa varieties (ramanas rose)	Deciduous; flowers in shades of pink, red and white in summer
Rosmarinus officinalis (rosemary)	Evergreen; blue flowers in summer
Santolina chamaecyparissus and *S. c.* 'Nana' (cotton lavender)	Evergreen; woolly silvery foliage; yellow flowers in summer
Senecio 'Sunshine'	Evergreen; silver-grey leaves; yellow flowers in summer
Spiraea x arguta (bridal wreath)	Deciduous; white flowers in spring
Stranvaesia davidiana	Evergreen; crimson berries in autumn
Symphoricarpos x chenaultii 'White Hedge' (snowberry)	Deciduous; white berries in autumn
Syringa microphylla 'Superba' (lilac)	Deciduous; rose-pink flowers, spring to autumn
Tamarix gallica (tamarisk)	Deciduous; plumes of pink feathery flowers in summer
Ulex europaeus 'Plenus' (double-flowered gorse)	Evergreen; semi-double yellow flowers in spring
V. tinus (laurustinus)	Evergreen; white flowers in winter and spring

Planting distance and pruning time	Special uses or conditions
18in (45cm) Early spring	As *O. avicennifolia*
24in (60cm) Late spring	Suitable for seaside gardens and chalky soils; needs shelter from cold winds
18in (45cm) Immediately after flowering	Dwarf hedge; grows well on chalk
18-24in (45-60cm) Early summer	Forms an impenetrable hedge
18in (45cm) Spring	Forms a low hedge
12in (30cm) Spring or early summer	Form a spiny dense hedge; tough and adaptable
24in (60cm) Early summer, after flowering	Needs acid soil; takes dappled shade
24in (60cm) Early summer, after flowering	Needs acid soil; takes dappled shade
24in (60cm) Spring, after flowering	Very hardy and adaptable
18in (45cm) Early spring	Very free flowering
18in (45cm) Early spring	Vigorous, very prickly, ideal for seaside gardens
18in (45cm) Summer, after flowering	Not suited to cold or exposed gardens
12in (30cm) Summer, after flowering	Dwarf hedge; needs well-drained soil
18in (45cm) Summer, after flowering	Dwarf hedge. Ideal for exposed and seaside gardens
18in (45cm) Spring, after flowering	Forms a fairly low hedge, about 4-5ft (1·2-1·5m)
18in (45cm) Late summer	Takes shade and pollution
18in (45cm) Summer	Forms a fairly low hedge about 4-5ft (1·2-1·5m)
24in (60cm) After flowering	Excellent for chalky soils
12in (30cm) Early spring	Ideal for seaside gardens and windy sites; not suitable for shallow chalk
18in (45cm) Spring, after flowering	Acid or neutral soil; ideal for poor dry soils, for seaside gardens and exposed sites; very spiny and dense
18in (45cm) Spring or early summer	Suitable for seaside gardens, windy sites and chalky soils

INTERNAL HEDGES AND SCREENS

Screening is useful in other places besides the main boundaries of a garden. Within the garden itself, the fruit or vegetable plot may be best screened off from the ornamental areas; other utility areas may need to be kept separate; and it is frequently effective to divide the garden so that the whole cannot be seen in one glance, therefore creating an element of surprise.

A FRUITING SCREEN

Trained tree fruits and soft fruits are ideal for creating a screen, particularly in small gardens where space for fruit growing may be at a premium. Not only is such a screen highly productive, but it is decorative as well, particularly when the plants are in flower but also when they are bearing fruits.

All the fruit trees described here are trained perfectly flat, in one plane, so they take up very little space. For supports one can use a trellis screen, or a system of posts and wires. Stout timber posts are inserted about 6ft (2m) apart, and they support strong galvanized wires 18-24in (45-60cm) apart, stretched tight by means of straining bolts. The height of these supports should be 6-8ft (1·8-2·4m).

Above: *Apple trees grown as fans make an effective and productive internal screen.*
Below: *Fruits can be grown in other forms for use as screens, such as cordon and espalier apples and pears. Plums, cherries and peaches may be trained as fans. Raspberries make a dense screen when established.*

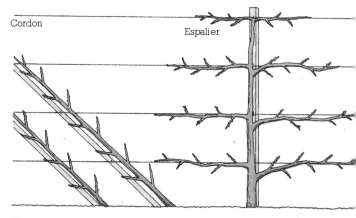

Cordon

Espalier

Cordons Apples and pears can be grown as cordons. These consist of a single main stem with short side shoots known as spurs which carry the fruits. The trees are bought partially trained and planted in a straight line against the support at an angle of about 45 degrees, 2½-3ft (75-90cm) apart. Each tree is supported with a bamboo cane, this being tied to the wires and the tree tied to the cane.

Espaliers Apples and pears can also be grown as espaliers. An espalier consists of a main central stem, from which grow pairs of opposite horizontal branches spaced about 18in (45cm) apart. As with cordons, the fruits are born on short side shoots or spurs on these branches. Each pair of branches is tied in to a horizontal wire. Plant espaliers 10ft (3m) apart.

Fan-trained fruits Plums, cherries and peaches can be grown as a fan shape, again with all the branches in one plane. The system of branches radiates from a short stem or trunk, each branch carrying the fruits. Plant fan-trained fruits 12-15ft (3·6-4·5m) apart.

Soft fruits Blackberries, loganberries and raspberries also make good productive screens and are again trained flat to a system of wires, or to trellis.

Blackberries and loganberries are planted 10ft (3m) apart, but as they are large plants you may find one of each sufficient. Raspberries are planted 18in (45cm) apart in a straight row. To supply the average family with fruit 12-18 plants will be needed.

Siting and care All of these fruits need an open, sunny position for optimum fruit production. Formative pruning, and thereafter regular annual pruning, will be needed. Cordons, espaliers and fans are supplied partially trained by the nurseryman. Pruning is a big subject and anyone contemplating growing these trained forms is advised to read it up in the specialist books.

CLIMBING PLANTS

Ornamental climbing plants can also be used to clothe trelliswork screens used to divide or hide parts of the garden. There is a wide range available, as indicated in the table on page 24. Evergreens provide all-year-round effect but deciduous climbers can also be used if you do not mind a more open screen in the autumn and winter. Climbers should be chosen carefully, for some need sunny positions while others thrive in shade.

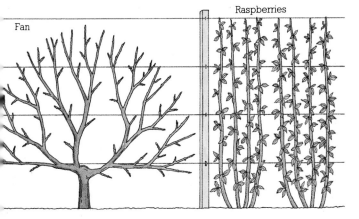

Fan

Raspberries

PLANTS FOR INTERNAL SCREENS

Name	Flowers/fruits/foliage
Apples	Deciduous; white and pink flowers in spring; fruits late summer and autumn
Blackberry	Deciduous; cut-leaved variety ('Oregon Thornless') has ferny foliage; fruits in late summer/early autumn
Ceanothus 'Delight'	Evergreen; deep blue flowers in spring
Cherry	Deciduous; attractive white flowers in spring; fruits in summer
Clematis x *jackmanii*	Deciduous; large violet-purple flowers in summer and autumn
Clematis, large-flowered garden hybrids	Deciduous; large flowers of many colours in spring and summer
Clematis montana rubens	Deciduous; rose-pink flowers in late spring/early summer
Hedera canariensis 'Variegata' (syn. 'Gloire de Marengo') (variegated Canary Island ivy)	Evergreen; large cream and green variegated leaves
Hedera helix varieties (common ivy)	Evergreen; small leaves, green or variegated
Jasminum nudiflorum (winter jasmine)	Deciduous; yellow flowers in autumn and winter
J. officinale (common white jasmine)	Deciduous; fragrant white flowers in early to late summer
Loganberry	Deciduous, fruits in summer
Lonicera periclymenum 'Belgica' (early Dutch honeysuckle)	Deciduous; cream flowers, flushed red-purple on outside, in spring and early summer
Peaches	Deciduous; attractive pink blossoms in spring; fruits in summer
Pears	Deciduous, attractive white flowers in spring, fruits in summer/early autumn
Plums	Deciduous; attractive white flowers in spring; fruits in summer
Raspberries	Deciduous; fruits in summer or
Rosa, climbing and rambling roses	Deciduous; large flowers in shades of pink, red, yellow, white etc in summer and autumn
Vitis 'Brant' (grape vine)	Deciduous; purple-black edible fruits in autumn; good autumn leaf colour
Wisteria floribunda 'Multijuga' (syn. 'Macrobotrys')	Deciduous; very long trusses of scented lilac flowers in spring

Pruning time	Special uses/conditions
Midsummer and early winter	Train as cordons or espaliers on trellis or wires; full sun
After fruiting in autumn	Train on trellis or posts and wires; full sun
After flowering if necessary	Train flat; needs shelter, full sun; avoid shallow chalk
Spring and late summer	Train as fan on trellis or posts and wires; full sun
Early spring	Keep roots shaded with stems in sun; good on chalk soils
Summer after flowering, or early spring, according to variety	Ditto
After flowering	Ditto
Late spring	Takes shade, full sun, pollution and any soil; slightly tender
Late spring	As *H. canariensis*, but hardy
Early spring	Adaptable; thrives in shade
Summer, after flowering	Needs plenty of sun for free flowering
Immediately after fruiting	Train on trellis or posts and wires; full sun
After flowering	Takes partial shade
Late spring and early autumn	Train as fan on trellis or posts and wires, full sun
Midsummer and early winter	Train as cordons or espaliers on trellis or posts and wires; full sun
Spring, summer and early autumn	Train as fan on trellis or posts and wires; full sun
Immediately after fruiting	Train on posts and wires, or trellis; full sun
Climbers early spring; ramblers immediately after flowering	Best in full sun; not recommended for shallow chalk soils
Winter and late spring/early summer	Full sun for best results, grows well on chalky soils
Late winter/early spring, and in midsummer	Best in full sun and moist soil

SCREENS FOR SPECIAL PURPOSES

Purpose	Recommended Screening
To muffle sound	Brick walls (double thickness bricks), concrete-block walls, concrete fences
For wind protection	Tall screens formed of trees; tall hedges; screen-block walling; trellis with climbers
Shade from the sun	Many small ornamental trees, perhaps planted near boundary, will provide shade. For immediate effect erect a timber pergola and grow climbers on it
To hide ugly views and to give complete privacy	Solid screens, such as close-boarded fencing, lapped fencing, brick or concrete walls; or evergreen hedges
To hide utility areas	Many options here: walls, solid or openwork; fencing panels; trellis with climbers; formal or informal hedges
To divide garden	Formal or informal hedges; trellis screens with climbers; screen-block walling
To provide a quickly grown living screen	Very fast-growing hedging plants like × *Cupressocyparis leylandii*; for tall screens quick-growing trees such as *Populus alba* and *P. nigra* 'Italica'
To build a quick artificial screen	Quickest to erect are interwoven or lapped fencing panels, and trellis panels
Supports for climbing plants	Ideally something they can cling to like trellis, screen-block walling, chain-link fencing, wire mesh fencing
To provide interest and/or colour all year round	Hedges should be evergreen. A mixed shrub border to form a boundary
Screening without reducing light	Trellis-work, screen-block walls
Wide living screens	Plant hedging plants in double staggered row
Very narrow living screen	Trellis with climbing plants or trained fruits
A living screen in very cold exposed areas	Hedges or tall screens of tough subjects such as *Crataegus monogyna*, *Fagus sylvatica*, *Hippophae rhamnoides*, *Larix decidua*, *Pinus nigra*, populus, *Prunus spinosa*, tamarix, *Taxus baccata*, ulex
A living screen for seaside gardens	Hedges or taller screens of *Atriplex halimus*, crataegus, cupressus, elaeagnus, escallonia, *Griselina littoralis*, hippophae, ilex, *laurus nobilis*, pinus, populus, *Quercus ilex*, salix, tamarix, ulex
A living screen to keep out dogs or other intruders	Need a dense, thick, spiny impenetrable hedge; e.g. berberis, crataegus, *Prunus spinosa*, *Rosa rugosa* varieties, ulex

Suggested Height	General Comments
At least 6ft (1·8m)	Seek professional advice when contemplating very high walls, 6ft (1·8m) and over
Trees allowed to grow to natural heights. Hedges, openwork walling and trellis: 6ft (1·8m) is a practical height	Trees only for very large gardens; hedges, etc, suited to smaller gardens
Small trees are of various heights: approximately 15-30ft (4·5-9m)	Do not plant too near hedges—reduced light results in poor growth
6ft (1·8m)	Bear in mind solid screens can result in wind turbulence in exposed situations
6ft (1·8m) is usually adequate	Oil tanks, coal bunkers, etc, are usually enclosed on three sides, the fourth kept open for access
6ft (1·8m) is usually adequate	May need a narrow screen so opt for trellis or screen-block walling
Hedge usually 6ft (1·8m) but will provide tall screen	Populus must be at least 100ft (30m) from buildings
6ft (1·8m) but lower screens available	Use metal post supports which are inserted in the ground
6ft (1·8m) will suit most climbers	Wires/trellis can also be fixed to solid walls and fences
Hedges 6-8ft (1·8-2·4m); shrubs are variable	A shrub border is space-consuming but provides flowers, foliage, berries and coloured stems
6ft (1·8m)	If you do not use climbers there will be good light penetration
6-8ft (1·8-2·4m)	Formal or informal hedges
6-8ft (1·8-2·4m)	Fruits can also be grown on a system of posts and wires
6-8ft (1·8-2·4m) for hedges; natural heights for tall screens	Plants may need artificial wind protection until established
6-8ft (1·8-2·4m) for hedges; natural heights for taller screens	These plants tolerate salt spray and protect the garden from this
6-8ft (1·8-2·4m)	Could plant in double staggered rows for really thick hedge

TALL SCREENS

If you have a very exposed or windy garden, desire complete privacy, or want to hide unsightly views, then you may wish to plant tall screens around your boundary, or along part of it. These are far taller than hedges and should only be considered if you have a really large garden.

PLANNING THE SITE

Tall screens are formed by planting a row of trees, or sometimes very tall shrubs, and allowing them to grow to their maximum height. Plenty of space must be available to allow this, for they will cast a great deal of shade and take a lot of moisture out of the soil for a distance of many yards. Also, one must be very conscious of root spread—with some subjects the roots spread great distances, and if they come in contact with the foundations of the house, or with drains or other underground services, they can cause a great deal of damage. So a tall screen of trees should never be planted near a house.

PLANTS USED

Mainly trees and conifers, deciduous and evergreen, are used to form tall screens. Examples are *Chamaecyparis lawsoniana* and varieties (Lawson cypress), evergreen conifers; × *Cupressocyparis leylandii* (Leyland cypress), evergreen conifer; *Populus alba* (white poplar), deciduous tree; *Populus nigra* 'Italica' (Lombardy poplar), deciduous tree; and *Thuja plicata* (western red cedar), evergreen conifer.

USES

Tall living screens are often used as windbreaks, particularly in flat, exposed parts of the country and in coastal areas. Strong, cold, drying winds, and salt-laden winds, can seriously

Above: *A shrub border backed by a tall screen of Lawson cypress,* Chamaecyparis lawsoniana. *Plenty of space is needed for this.*

affect the growth of many plants, and therefore limit the types of plants grown in a garden. Therefore it is a good idea to try to reduce windy conditions if possible.

A living screen of trees or tall shrubs is far better than a solid screen (such as a tall wall), for it filters the wind and slows it down. A solid screen stops the wind in its tracks: or rather, it rushes upwards, over the screen and plunges downwards on the other side. Such turbulence can result in great damage to plants.

WINDBREAKS

When a living screen is to be used as a windbreak it should be planted at right angles to the direction of the wind. A tall screen will reduce the force of the wind (on the leeward side) for a distance approximately 20 times greater than its height. Thus, a 30ft (9m) high screen will ensure calm conditions for a length of about 600ft (182m).

MIXED PLANTING

Of course, there is no need to limit yourself to only one type of tree or conifer. To create a more pleasing picture you could mix several kinds, such as different sorts of deciduous trees with evergreen conifers. You could plant each variety in a 'block' of several trees or shrubs. A solid row of evergreen conifers could result in a very heavy, closed-in atmosphere.

If the bottom of a living screen is open (in other words devoid of branches) and allows wind to rush through, plant a row of tough ornamental shrubs in front of it to fill the gap.

Below: *A tall screen of dark green conifers not only gives protection from wind, but forms a good background for plants.*

SIZES

When planted close together trees and conifers tend to grow upwards rather than outwards and so do not necessarily spread to any great extent. Nevertheless the spread will still be greater than, say, a normal hedge. For instance, *Chamaecyparis lawsoniana* and its varieties can spread to at least 10-12ft (3-3·6m); × *Cupressocyparis leylandii* to 15ft (4·5m); *Populus alba* to 15-20ft (4·5-6m); and *P. nigra* 'Italica' to 8ft (2·4m), this being one of the narrowest screening trees. Poplars have an enormous root spread, though, and should not be planted closer than 100ft (30m) from buildings.

Heights vary according to subject, but bear in mind that screens can be lopped after some years if you want to curtail height (although the result is not particularly attractive). *Chamaecyparis lawsoniana* and *Populus alba* can attain 40ft (12m), and × *Cupressocyparis leylandii* and *Populus nigra* 'Italica' may reach 50ft (15m).

PLANTS FOR TALL SCREENS

Tall screens for wind protection or privacy can be created with many kinds of trees, deciduous and evergreen, broad-leaved and coniferous. Most are fairly fast growing, as can be seen from the table, where expected heights after 20 years have been given. It is difficult to give ultimate heights for these trees as this can depend so much on soil conditions and climate.

Name	Foliage/habit
Chamaecyparis lawsoniana (Lawson cypress)	Evergreen; sprays of medium green foliage
X *Cupressocyparis leylandii* (Leyland cypress)	Evergreen; sprays of deep green foliage
Cupressus macrocarpa (Monterey cypress)	Evergreen; bright green foliage
Larix decidua (European larch)	Deciduous; light green foliage, pleasing autumn colour
Picea abies (Norway spruce)	Evergreen; bright green needles
Pinus nigra (Austrian pine)	Evergreen; deep green needles
P.n. maritima (Corsican pine)	Evergreen; grey-green needles
P. radiata (Monterey pine)	Evergreen; bright green needles
Populus alba (white poplar)	Deciduous; leaves white below, autumn colour yellow
P. canescens (poplar)	Deciduous; leaves grey-white below; autumn colour yellow
P. tremula (aspen)	Deciduous; leaves tremble in the slightest breeze; autumn colour yellow
Quercus ilex (evergreen oak)	Evergreen; deep green glossy leaves
Q. robur (common or English oak)	Deciduous; lobed, medium green leaves
Salix alba (white willow)	Deciduous; leaves have silvery undersides
S. caprea (goat willow)	Deciduous; rounded leaves, grey or yellow catkins in spring
Sorbus aria (whitebeam)	Deciduous; greyish oval leaves, white below; good autumn colour
Thuja plicata (western red cedar)	Evergreen; flat sprays of bright green, glossy foliage
Tilia cordata (small-leaved lime)	Deciduous; deep green leaves, paler below
Tsuga canadensis (eastern hemlock)	Evergreen; short narrow needles with white bands below

All of these plants can be planted 6-8ft (1·8-2·4m) apart to form a screen, either in single or double staggered rows.

If, at a later date, it is felt that they need thinning out, then by all means do so. But to start with it is important to plant closely to give a quick effect.

If eventually the screen becomes bare at the base, plant a line of shrubs in front of it.

Expected height after 20 years	Special uses/conditions
40ft (12m)	Will not take extreme exposure
50ft (15m)	Suitable for seaside gardens and very chalky soils
50ft (15m)	Suited only to mild areas and seaside gardens
50ft (15m)	Not suitable for shallow chalk soils; ideal for cold or exposed sites
50ft (15m)	Suitable for chalk soils
35ft (10m)	Ideal for seaside gardens, very exposed sites and for chalky soils
40ft (12m)	Very adaptable; suitable for cold exposed areas and seaside gardens
50ft (15m)	Grow in mild areas and seaside gardens
40ft (12m)	Grows well in wet soils and seaside gardens
30-50ft (9-15m)	Ditto
30ft (9m)	Ditto
20ft (6m)	Ideal for seaside gardens and chalky soils
12-18ft (3·6-5·4m)	Grows well in cold or exposed areas; not recommended for shallow chalk soils
40ft (12m)	Suited to very cold or exposed areas, seaside gardens and wet soils
20-25ft (6-7·6m)	
20ft (6m)	Suited to very cold or exposed sites, seaside gardens, chalky soils and industrial pollution
50ft (15m)	Not suited to very exposed sites; best in moist soil but takes shallow chalk
30ft (9m)	Suitable for cold exposed areas and polluted air
30ft (9m)	Suitable for cold or exposed sites; takes shade; not recommended for shallow chalk

As with any plants supplied by garden centres and nurseries, the quality of hedging and screening plants varies, so it pays to shop around for top quality. The better the plants, the faster they will establish.

GARDEN CENTRE BUYING

The most convenient place to buy hedging and screening plants is in a local garden centre. The plants are usually supplied in containers, such as flexible polythene bags. In garden centres you can inspect plants closely for quality.

How to choose top-quality plants:
● They should be well-branched right down to the base, especially in the case of hedging plants.
● If conifers are bare at the base they will be no good for hedging, as they will never make new growth in this area.
● Foliage should look generally healthy and not be spotted or marked with brown patches. Leaves should not be brown at the edges.
● Plants should not be showing any signs of pests and diseases.
● Climbing plants should be tied in to bamboo canes or other forms of support and should not have tangled growth.
● Hedging plants should be no more than about 2ft (60cm) in height. Trees for tall screens may be taller but ideally go for really young specimens known as whips (consisting of a single stem without side branches or feathers, in the case of broad-leaved trees).
● The compost in the containers should be moist—if it has dried out this can result in leaf drop later on, especially in the case of conifers and evergreen shrubs.
● Plants should be well-established in their containers, with perhaps a little root showing through the bottom. But they should not be pot-bound (when the pot is packed full of roots) as this can delay establishment of the hedge after planting.

NURSERY BUYING

You may also be able to buy plants from a local nursery, perhaps plants which have been grown in the field. In this instance they may be supplied 'bare-rooted' if deciduous plants; or 'rootballed', with a ball of soil around the roots, held in place with, say, hessian or plastic mesh, in the case of evergreen shrubs and conifers. Plants may work out cheaper than containerized specimens from a garden centre. As regards quality, consider the points outlined above before parting with your money.

Below: *Make sure that the plants are well established in containers and that the compost is moist. If dry, leaf drop can occur.*

It is possible to buy mail-order from nurseries, who often advertise in the gardening and national press. Try to find a well-known, reputable company who can be relied upon to supply top-quality plants, preferably a tree and shrub specialist. Generally it is best to avoid companies advertising 'special offers' or who use such terms as 'fantastic value'. The plants may be very small. You only get what you pay for!

WHEN TO BUY PLANTS

Try to buy as near planting time as possible, as it is best to get plants established quickly, especially in the case of bare-rooted or rootballed plants.

Evergreens (including conifers) can be planted in September/October, or in April/May, especially rootballed specimens. Containerized evergreens can be planted throughout spring, summer and early autumn.

Deciduous subjects are planted between November and March if bare-rooted; or at any time when the ground is in a suitable state if in containers.

If you are buying from a mail-order company be sure to order in good time: for example, order in spring or summer for autumn delivery; summer for winter delivery; and autumn or winter for spring delivery. The order forms supplied with catalogues generally indicate the most suitable times for placing orders to guarantee delivery at the time required.

PLANTING HEDGES

A hedge is a long-term feature and in the early years it is important that it grows steadily and vigorously. Thorough soil preparation is therefore essential before planting.

SITING THE HEDGE

A common mistake is to plant a hedge far too close to the boundary line, with the result that it spreads onto the pavement or neighbour's garden. You must therefore estimate the eventual width of the hedge (whether it is a formal or informal hedge), then plant your row of hedging plants at least half this width from the boundary line.

GROUND PREPARATION

First mark out with garden lines a strip of ground 3-4ft (1-1·2m) wide. Then dig the strip, at the same time adding bulky organic matter to each trench, such as well-rotted farmyard manure, garden compost, peat, leafmould, spent hops, mushroom compost or pulverized bark. A quarter of a barrowload per trench will not be too much.

First take out a 2ft (60cm) wide trench, the depth of the spade, across one end of the strip and deposit the soil at the other end, to fill in the final trench. Then break up the bottom of the trench to the depth of a fork and spread a layer of organic matter over it. Move back and take out another 2ft (60cm) wide trench, throwing the soil forward into the first. Break up the bottom and add organic matter. Continue in this way to the end of the strip.

If the site is infested with perennial weeds kill these off with glyphosate weedkiller before digging.

1

2

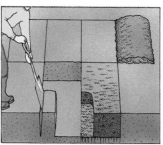

3

4

Above: Double digging. First take out a trench 2ft (60cm) wide (1). Then dig over the bottom to the full depth of the spade or fork and add bulky organic matter (2). Now take out a second trench, throwing the soil forward into the first one (3). Again dig the soil in the bottom (4). Continue in this way down the plot.

It is best to allow the dug site to settle, a few months if possible.

Just before planting apply a general-purpose fertilizer, such as Growmore, at 4oz per square yard (113 grammes per square metre). Then break down the roughly dug soil to a reasonably fine tilth and firm it well by treading with your heels.

PLANTING TIMES

Evergreen hedging plants, including conifers, are ideally planted either in September/ October or in April/May. This would certainly apply to root-balled plants lifted from the open ground. Containerized evergreens could, though, be planted throughout spring, summer and early autumn.

Deciduous hedging plants are planted between November and March if they are bare-rooted (provided the ground is not excessively wet or frozen), but if they are in containers planting can be undertaken at any time of year if ground conditions are suitable.

PLANTING TECHNIQUES

Generally a single line of plants is sufficient, but if you want a really wide hedge, for example, well in excess of 3ft (1m), then plant a double staggered row, the rows being 15in (38cm) apart. Planting distances for hedging plants are given on pages 12-15 and 18-21. Put down a garden line to ensure you plant in a straight row.

CONTAINERIZED PLANTING

Containerized hedging plants are generally supplied in flexible polythene bags. To remove, slit down one side and underneath and peel off. Do not disturb the rootball; place in a hole slightly wider than the ball, and of sufficient depth that when planting is completed the top of

the rootball is about ½in (12mm) below the surface of the surrounding soil. Work fine soil into the space between rootball and sides of hole, and firm really well with your heels.

BARE-ROOTED PLANTING

If planting bare-rooted plants, first trim back any broken or damaged roots with secateurs. Take out a hole sufficiently large to allow the roots to be spread out to their full extent. Planting depth should be to the soil mark, which will be found near the base of the stem. Return some fine soil over the roots and then gently shake the plant up and down to work the soil well between the roots. Then return more soil, firming with your heels as you proceed, until the hole is filled in. These planting details also apply to tall screens.

Top: *Bare-rooted plants should have damaged or broken roots trimmed back.*
Above: *Plant against a line and firm in the plants thoroughly.*

CARE AFTER PLANTING

Hedges or screens must not be forgotten and left to their own devices after planting, or they may be slow to establish and could even die on you. Lavish care and attention on them and they will repay you by quickly establishing and making new top growth.

ESTABLISHMENT

It is worth bearing in mind that hedges establish much more quickly, and grow more strongly, if grass is not allowed to grow right up to the stems. If a hedge is used as an internal garden divider across a lawn, a strip of bare soil, about 18in (45cm) wide, should be left along each side of the hedge. Once the hedge has reached its desired height, the grass can be allowed to grow up to the hedge.

STAKING

Most hedging and screening plants do not need staking, especially if, as recommended, you use small plants. However, some do appreciate supports in their early years, particularly shallow-rooted kinds, such as *Cupressus macrocarpa,* × *Cupressocyparis leylandii* and crataegus. This is especially important if your garden is subjected to strong winds, for if plants are lashed around by gales they may have difficulty rooting.

Small plants can be supported by supplying each one with a stout bamboo cane and tying it in with soft garden string. Or, if there are many plants to support, a system of posts and horizontal wires (such as telephone cable) may be rigged up and the plants tied to the wires. A combination of the two may also be used, the canes being tied to the wires.

Plants will not need supports for more than two years after planting, for if they come to rely on them for too long they may not make adequate anchoring roots.

Above: *A young* Thuja plicata *hedge which has been kept weed-free and watered as required.*

WIND PROTECTION

It is important to protect some newly planted hedging and screening plants from cold drying winds, which can scorch and dry out the foliage, and even result in their death. Evergreen shrubs and conifers, especially, will need wind protection in open, exposed areas. However, within one or two years from planting they toughen up and therefore protection may not be needed. The best advice, though, is to keep an eye on the plants and if protection needs to be continued for a further period, then provide it.

Generally, plants need protection only from late autumn to mid-spring each year, but of course this can depend on the area—if it is prone to cold drying winds at any time of year, then the protection should be left in place until the plants are really well established and growing strongly.

Wind protection can simply consist of a screen of windbreak netting on stout canes or posts, taller than the plants, and within 2-3ft (60-90cm) of them. Erect it on the windward side. Plastic-mesh windbreak netting is available from garden centres.

PREVENTING WATER LOSS

Newly planted evergreen shrubs and conifers are prone to rapid loss of moisture through their leaves, quicker than they take it up from the soil because fine 'drinking' roots will not have established. Moisture loss is greatest in dry weather, especially in combination with drying winds.

You must prevent rapid loss of moisture, or plants may be slow to establish and could even die. So immediately after planting evergreen shrubs and conifers spray them with a proprietary

Below: *Newly planted subjects should be watered heavily when the soil is becoming dry.*

anti-transpirant spray (available from garden centres in aerosol form). Repeat if necessary (after heavy rain) for a period of six weeks. Alternatively, spray plants daily with plain water (but not if it is raining) for a period of six weeks.

WATERING

Do not let newly planted subjects dry out at the roots. Water heavily whenever the top inch of so of the soil starts drying out. This should be continued for the first year after planting, and indeed until the hedge or screen is really well-established (for instance, until a hedge has gained its required height). See pages 42-43 for further details of watering established hedges.

MULCHING

Immediately after planting it is a good idea to apply a mulch (a layer of organic matter) over the soil surface to prevent rapid drying out of the soil and growth of annual weeds. Spread a layer about 2in (5cm) deep of garden compost, peat, pulverized bark or well-rotted manure along either side of the hedge and between the plants, but not right up to the stems. Make sure the soil is thoroughly moist.

TRAINING NEW HEDGES

All too often hedges are neglected after planting, with the result that in time they become decidedly bedraggled, or too large. One of the main tasks is clipping, or trimming. This should start immediately after planting.

ESSENTIAL TOOLS

The majority of hedging plants have small leaves, and therefore formal hedges can be trimmed with ordinary garden shears or with an electric hedge trimmer. Examples are privet (*Ligustrum ovalifolium*), beech and hornbeam (*Fagus sylvatica* and *Carpinus betulus*), Chinese honeysuckle (*Lonicera nitida*) and box (*Buxus sempervirens*). Shears or electric trimmers can also be used for conifer hedges.

However, it is not recommended that either of these tools are used on formal hedges of large-leaved hedging plants, such as laurel (*Prunus laurocerasus*) as they cut the leaves in half. This looks unsightly, particularly when, eventually, the cut edges turn brown. Although it may seem laborious and time-consuming, such hedges are best cut with a pair of secateurs, cutting each shoot individually. Informal hedges should also be trimmed with secateurs, whether the plants are small- or large-leaved.

INITIAL TRAINING

Formal deciduous hedges Initial training should aim to encourage side branching, as dense, bushy growth is needed, particularly from the base of the hedge. This area is especially important and it is here that trouble is most likely to occur. This is because, understandably, most hedges are allowed to attain the required height as quickly as they will grow. But, in doing so, the foliage at the base of the hedge is sacrificed as most of the plants' energy is confined to

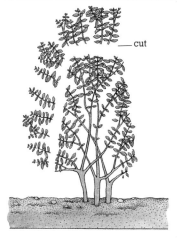

Above: *Immediately after planting formal deciduous hedges, severely reduce top and side growth.*

producing extension growth.

Therefore, immediately after planting in winter, for all plants except conifers and some broad-leaved evergreens, reduce all growth to half to two thirds of its length—both leading shoots and side shoots. Leading shoots, or leaders, are those which grow straight up from the central stem or trunk and are usually vertical.

Any side shoots present at this stage will be quite short already, but even so, should be cut back. Such cutting may seem drastic, but it does eventually ensure the dense growth required, as it stimulates buds into growth which would otherwise have remained dormant, and so produces a thicker cover.

At this stage, it will be possible to make cuts individually with secateurs, and such cuts should be immediately above a bud. If a shoot is growing very strongly, much more so than its fellows, cut back by half, but cut the weak, short ones so as to remove two thirds of their length.
Formal conifer hedges This treatment is not recommended for conifer hedges, though, as these bush out quite naturally. However, any over-long or untidy

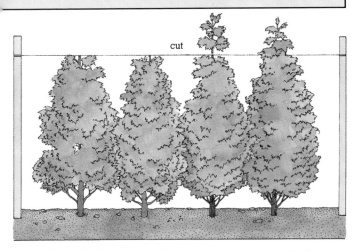

cut

Above: *When leading shoots of conifers have slightly exceeded desired height, cut them back.*

side shoots could be trimmed back to bring them into line with the rest of the hedge.

Formal slow-growing broad-leaved evergreen hedges These include such subjects as holly, laurel and aucuba, and they are best treated in the same way as the conifers.

Informal hedges These should also be cut back hard immediately after they are planted in winter, in the same way as for deciduous formal hedges. A good bushy base is wanted just as much as with a formal hedge, perhaps more so, since informal hedges are grown for their flowers.

SECOND-YEAR AND SUBSEQUENT TREATMENTS

Formal deciduous hedges Allow these to reach the desired height in stages by cutting back the new growth of the leading shoots by about half when this growth is 8-12in (200-300mm) long. Do this in summer, but no later than the end of late summer, otherwise any new growth may not be sufficiently ripe to withstand the winter cold without being injured and thereby allowing entry for fungal and other

diseases. In winter, trim the side shoots back hard.

Conifer and broad-leaved evergreen hedges Continue to retain the leading shoots, and tidy the side shoots as required in late summer or winter. When the leading shoots are 6-12in (150-300mm) above the desired height, cut them back to just above the side shoots which are 6in (150mm) below the height required.

Informal hedges Leave these to grow in subsequent years after the initial cutting back. But if it is found that they are not making much side growth, cut back the leading shoots again by about half the length of their new growth in the second winter, and even in the third, if it appears to be necessary. Although it may mean losing a season's flowers in some cases, it is better to do this and ensure a well-clothed hedge in future.

After about three growing seasons, the hedge should be growing well enough for its regular trimming to be started. This should always be done between spring and early autumn, and the winter trimming of the formative years will no longer be required. In order to ensure a really straight top to a formal hedge, use a garden line or length of string as a guide, running it along one side of the hedge at the desired ultimate height.

ROUTINE TRIMMING AND PRUNING

After initial training, hedges, especially formal ones, need regular trimming, maybe once of more each year. Climbing plants which are used for screening will also need regular pruning. The times to trim or prune are given in the plant lists.

FORMAL HEDGES

Once a hedge has ben fully trained, only light trimming will be needed: only the new shoots should be trimmed, rather than the older wood.

Some hedging plants are fast growers and need trimming several times during the growing season to keep them looking neat and tidy and to maintain dense growth. If the growth of these is allowed to become too long it is more difficult to cut.

FAST AND SLOW GROWERS

The fastest-growing hedging plants are privet (ligustrum) which needs clipping once a month in the growing season; Chinese honeysuckle (*Lonicera nitida*), which needs to be trimmed at similar intervals; box (*Buxus sempervirens*), which, although not as fast as the first two, nevertheless needs several clippings during the growing

Above: *Although slow, secateurs make a good job of trimming conifer hedges like the Lawson cypress and varieties.*
Below left: *Side shoots of wisteria are pruned back to within 6in (150mm) of the main stems in mid-summer.*
Below right: *Then in late winter or early spring they are shortened to two buds. Use sharp secateurs.*

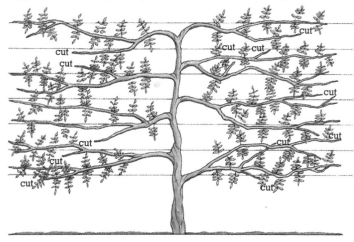

season if it is to look really neat, and hawthorn (crataegus), which generally needs several trims. Most other formal hedging plants need only one cut per year, usually in summer, but by all means give another trim if it appears necessary, for it will certainly do no harm provided it is no later than early autumn.

INFORMAL HEDGES

These are trimmed, if necessary, after flowering, though with late-summer-flowering species, you should trim a long time after they have flowered in the following spring. Generally reduce in length only over-long or particularly straggly shoots. Do not trim the entire hedge, or you will ruin the natural shape and probably end up with a formal hedge, with few flowers in subsequent years. Use secateurs for tidying up informal hedges.

PRUNING CLIMBERS

Ceanothus 'Delight'—cut back side shoots but not into older wood which forms the framework.
Clematis × *jackmanii*—to prevent a tangled mass of growth the previous year's shoots can be shortened to growth buds or new shoots.

Clematis, large-flowered garden hybrids—as for *C.* × *jackmanii.*
Clematis montana rubens—cut out some of the older stems by one-half to two-thirds, to prevent a tangled mass of growth.
Hedera species and cultivars—cut the side shoots hard back almost to the main stems, removing most of the foliage, to reduce weight. They will soon make plenty of new foliage.
Jasminum nudiflorum—cut back the old flowered side shoots almost to the main stems.
Jasminum officinale—cut one or two of the oldest stems right out each year to prevent the development of a tangled mass of growth.
Lonicera periclymenum 'Belgica'—cut out some of the older stems by one-half to two-thirds.
Rosa, climbing cultivars—cut back side shoots to within one to three buds of the main stems.
Rosa, rambling cultivars—with those that produce new shoots near the base, cut the old flowered stems right out.
Vitis 'Brant'—cut back side shoots to within one or two buds of the main stems.
Wisteria floribunda 'Multijuga' (also known as 'Macrobotrys')—cut back side shoots in mid-summer to within 6in (150mm) of the main stems, and in late winter/early spring shorten them to two buds.

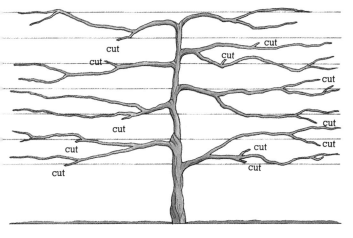

HEDGE CARE

Like other garden plants, hedges respond to regular feeding, watering and so on, contrary to popular belief. Many hedges receive no treatment other than trimming, and consequently do not look in the peak of health.

WATERING

It often comes as a surprise to many people to learn that hedges need watering regularly in dry periods just as much as other plants. If a hedge is allowed to suffer from dryness at the roots top growth will slow down. Hedges take up a great amount of water in dry weather so nearby plants will also need extra water.

It is possible to use a garden sprinkler to water hedges—an oscillating or rotary type. But perhaps even more effective is a seep hose laid alongside the hedge, which emits a fine, gentle spray of water along its length.

Start watering when the top 1in (25mm) of soil has become dry. A large quantity of water needs to be applied each time so that it penetrates the soil to a depth of at least 6in (150mm). This means applying the equivalent of 1in (25mm) of rain, which equals 5 gallons per square yard (27 litres per m²). This can be measured by placing some empty cans in the area to be watered: when they have 1in (25mm) of water in the bottom you know sufficient has been applied.

As a further test, about one hour after watering dig a hole 6in (150mm) deep. If the soil is moist at the bottom, sufficient water has been applied; if dry, turn on the sprinkler again.

FEEDING

In the spring apply a topdressing of general-purpose or flower-garden fertilizer, well balanced in the major plant foods nitrogen, phosphorus and potash. Sprinkle it along each side of the hedge if possible, in a band about 3ft

Above: *Even established hedges benefit from heavy watering in dry weather.*
Below: *For weedkilling under hedges, use a dribble bar.*

(900mm) wide, at a rate of 4oz per square yard (113g per m²). Lightly hoe or fork it into the surface, and if the soil is dry, water it in thoroughly.

Foliar feeds can be beneficial in summer if growth seems to be poor. This involves applying a liquid fertilizer to the leaves and it is very quickly absorbed by the plants. Ideally use a liquid fertilizer which is high in nitrogen, as this food stimulates vegetative growth. The fertilizer is most easily applied with a garden pressure sprayer, using a coarse spray. A foliar feed can be repeated several times during the summer if considered necessary.

MULCHING

This has already been discussed under Care After Planting, page 36. The purpose is to prevent rapid drying out of the soil and to suppress the growth of annual weeds. Top up the mulch annually if necessary, in the spring. It is good practice to keep a hedge permanently mulched, no matter how old it is.

Below: *Mulching a new hedge with peat. This layer helps to prevent rapid drying out of the soil and also suppresses the growth of annual weeds. Apply to moist soil.*

WEED CONTROL UNDER THE HEDGE

Many different weeds can become established under the hedge and they compete with it for moisture, foods and light. Annual weeds can be pulled out by hand and perennial kinds dug out with a hand fork, including the roots. You may be able to hoe off seedling weeds: a draw hoe is easier to use under a hedge than a Dutch hoe.

There are several weedkillers that can be used under hedges, provided they do not come into contact with the leaves of the hedge. For instance, paraquat is extremely effective for controlling annual weeds. Propachlor granules, sprinkled over weed-free soil, will prevent growth of annual weeds for up to eight weeks.

Glyphosate is very effective in controlling perennial weeds such as ground elder and couch grass. If there are only a few perennial weeds under the hedge, this weedkiller could be applied to individual weeds, using a 'spot' applicator.

Paraquat and glyphosate are best applied with a watering can fitted with a dribble bar, to prevent contact with the hedge foliage, rather than with a garden pressure sprayer.

HEDGE CARE

Apart from watering, feeding, mulching, training and trimming, general grooming can do nothing but good. So give some attention to the following aspects of hedge care.

REMOVING DEAD MATERIAL

Due to lack of light, shoots often eventually die off inside an established hedge. It is advisable to remove this dead wood as it can encourage diseases such as coral spot (appears as coral-coloured spots on the bark) which may spread to healthy wood. Removal of dead wood is best undertaken when the hedge is in leaf as then it is more easily seen. Do not just break it out, but make clean cuts with secateurs, right back to the main stems or branches.

Shoots are inclined to die off at the base of the hedge, too, if weeds are allowed to grow, as they prevent full light from reaching the bottom of the hedge.

REMOVING SNOW

If snow builds up on top of a hedge it can split it asunder due to the sheer weight. Invariably when this happens the hedge never regains its original shape, even though the stems or branches may not necessarily be broken. So gently dislodge snow before it builds up too much, using any handy implement such as a broom handle. Do not be too rough when doing this, or side shoots could be damaged.

HOW TO TREAT PHYSICAL DAMAGE

Hedges forming front boundaries are, of course, prone to physical damage—from vandalism, for example, although one always

Below: *Do not allow snow to build up on top of a hedge, as it can cause considerable damage. Gently dislodge it with a broom handle—don't be too rough!*

hopes this will not occur. But what do you do if stems are broken? They should be cut back beyond the damage, using secateurs or loppers to ensure really clean cuts, and the wounds treated with a proprietary pruning compound. Many hedging plants produce new growth from old wood (see Renovating Old Hedges, pages 46-47), so eventually any gaps will be filled in. Of course, there is nothing that can be done in the interim to reduce the unsightliness of such damage.

If any of the hedging plants have been broken off at ground level it would be better to replace them with new plants, after first thoroughly preparing the soil as described on pages 34-35.

DEALING WITH POLLUTION

Hedges in industrial areas, or near busy roads, are subjected to pollution. a layer of grime can build up on the leaves,

Above: *Dead wood should always be removed from hedges as it can encourage diseases such as coral spot. Do this job when the hedge is in leaf, when the dead wood can be easily seen.*

impairing their functions and so retarding the growth of the hedge. Apart from this, a soiled hedge is unsightly.

Acid rain can also result in unsightly spots or other marks on the leaves.

If hedges are affected by pollution it is recommended that they are literally washed off frequently. This is easily achieved by forcefully spraying them with a hosepipe fitted with one of the adjustable spray nozzles.

If you are in an area prone to pollution and contemplating planting a hedge, it would be advisable to choose a deciduous subject, so that when the leaves fall in the autumn the grime falls away with them.

RENOVATING OLD HEDGES

Whether hedges have been cared for properly, or have been neglected, they may eventually become too large and need to be reduced in height and width. Sometimes old hedges die out in patches. Parts of a hedge can be killed by severe frosts. All these problems can be overcome.

REDUCING THE SIZE OF A HEDGE

If height as well as spread needs to be reduced, carry out the operation over a period of two to three years. It is a mistake to hand prune a hedge in one operation as this will give it a great shock and it may be slow to recover. For example, in year one reduce the height; in year two cut back one side; and in year three cut back the other side.

It is best to use long-handled heavy duty loppers for this type of pruning, for invariably one will be cutting into quite thick wood.

Many of the hedging plants recommended in the tables can be cut hard by as much as half their height and/or spread, right into the old thick wood, and they will freely produce new growth from this. The best time to carry out hard pruning is spring, just before or just as growth is starting.

PLANTS WHICH CAN BE CUT BACK HARD

Formal hedges: Aucuba, buxus (box), carpinus (hornbeam), corylus (hazel), crataegus (hawthorn), elaeagnus, euonymus, fagus (beech), griselinia, ilex (holly), laurus (sweet bay), ligustrum (privet), *Lonicera nitida*, pittosporum, *Prunus cerasifera (cherry plum), P. laurocerasus (laurel), P. lusitanica (Portugal laurel), P. spinosa (blackthorn)*, pyracantha (firethorn), rhododendron, taxus (yew) and *Viburnum tinus (laurustinis)*.
Informal hedges: Atriplex, camellia, cotoneaster, escallonia, forsythia, fuschia, hebe, hippophae

Top: *The author reducing the height of his laurel hedge, using long-handled heavy-duty loppers.* **Above:** *After the operation! The width will be reduced in the following year so that the hedge does not receive too great a shock.*

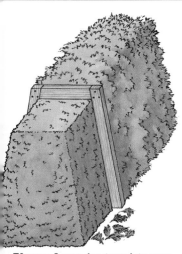

Above: *A wooden template, very easily made at home, can be used to define the desired shape when cutting back an old neglected overgrown hedge. The wedge shape—broad at the base—is recommended for formal hedges.*

(sea buckthorn), hydrangea, olearia (daisy bush), × osmarea, philadelphus (mock orange blossom), potentilla (shrubby cinquefoil), ribes (flowering currant), rosa, santolina (cotton holder), senecio, spiraea, stranvaesia, symphoricarpos (snowberry), syringa (lilac), tamarix, ulex (gorse) and *Viburnum opulus* (guelder rose).

Others, such as rosemary, lavender, etc, are best replaced if they become too large, straggly or unshapely.

On no account should conifer hedges (with the exception of taxus) be cut back hard, as generally these will not produce new growth from the old wood. If they have grown too large for your garden, they will have to be replaced. However, the tops of tall conifer screens can be lopped if desired, although the result is not very attractive and therefore not really recommended. Tops of tall broad-leaved screens can sometimes be lopped with less damage to the aesthetic effect.

HEDGES DYING OUT IN PLACES

This can be most annoying, for it ruins the hedge's appearance.

Cupressus macrocarpa can suddenly die in places, particularly if it is trimmed or pruned too hard. *Lonicera nitida* can lose foliage from the older and lower branches at the base and can also die out altogether. With lonicera hard pruning, to as low as 6in (150mm) of ground level, may help to revive it.

If the complete hedge dies, say slowly from one end to the other, then suspect honey fungus (see table of diseases on page 50). Privet (ligustrum) is particularly prone to this disease.

If gaps do appear in the hedge because plants have died out (provided the cause is not honey fungus) try replacing with young specimens, but first thoroughly prepare the planting site to give them a good start. If honey fungus is the problem then it would not be advisable to replant with hedging. Consider instead an artificial screen of some kind.

LAYING HEDGES

An old hedge which has been in place many years may not be producing much new growth and is often bare at the base as well. Both problems can be remedied by laying the hedge. This involves cutting many stems right out near to ground level. The remainder have a long slanting cut made partially through them, starting about 1ft (30cm) above soil level, and are then bent over at an angle of 45° and woven around slanting stakes put in behind the hedge at right angles to the stems being laid. The retained stems should be chosen for even spacing, and those cut right down hard will sprout new growth low down. The time to do this is in the winter. Most common deciduous hedging plants can be treated and one or two evergreens, such as holly, but not conifers.

Fortunately hedging plants do not suffer from too many insect pests, but there are a few to watch out for. If they are allowed to build up they could weaken the growth of the hedge.

The accompanying table lists the most likely insect and other pests of hedges. In small numbers they will probably do little harm to well-established hedges; it is when they build up into large colonies that they result in a weakening effect. Therefore it is sensible to take remedial action as soon as any pest is seen.

A range of suitable insecticides is recommended in the table and these are most easily applied with a garden pressure sprayer, using a medium or coarse spray to ensure every part of the hedge is wetted. It is particularly important to spray the undersides of the leaves and the shoot tips, for many pests congregate and feed in these areas.

Always follow the manufacturer's instructions on using insecticides, and do not spray during periods of strong sunshine or on a windy day.

Of the pests listed, aphids and caterpillars of various kinds are probably the most common.

Right: *Caterpillars have huge appetites, and can ruin a hedge.*

Name	Description/damage
Aphids (greenfly, blackfly etc)	Pinhead-size bugs which congregate on shoot tips and suck the sap
Beetle, raspberry	White maggots which feed inside the fruits
Capsid bugs	Small green fast-moving bugs which suck the sap of plants
Caterpillars	Various kinds will eat the leaves of plants. They are generally green or brown
Galls	These are abnormal growths or swellings on leaves, branches or stems and are caused by various insects or mites
Mite, red spider	Tiny spider-like creatures barely visible with naked eye. Suck sap and cause fine pale mottling on leaves
Moth, codlin	Grubs feed inside fruits
Moth, goat or leopard	Large caterpillars feed inside branches and trunks, killing either branches or whole plants
Moth, tortrix	Small caterpillars which feed on leaves and spin them together
Sawflies	Small caterpillars which feed on apple fruits and on leaves; can completely defoliate plants
Scale insects	Immobile tiny scale-like insects generally brown, which suck the sap from stems
Weevils	Small beetle-like insects, black or brown, with long 'snouts', which eat notches out of leaf edges

Plants attacked	Control
Shrubs, roses and fruits	Spray with malathion, dimetholate, or permethrin plus heptenophos
Raspberries and blackberries	Spray or dust with derris at petal fall and repeat at early fruit stage
Mainly fruits; also some shrubs, especially hydrangea, fuchsia	Spray, in spring, with HCH (BHC), malathion or dimethoate
Many shrubs and fruits	Spray with derris, or permethrin plus heptenophos
Many, especially willow, oak and yew	Generally not harmful so control not needed
Fruits and many shrubs	Spray with dimethoate or malathion
Apples	Spray with permethrin plus heptenophos
Many trees and shrubs, but attacks are only occasional	Cut off and burn dying branches
Fruits, roses, trees and shrubs	Spray with derris, or permethrin plus heptenophos
Fruits and roses	Spray them with dimethoate, or permethrin plus heptenophos
Fruits and shrubs, especially beech, sweet bay	Spray with dimethoate, or permethrin plus heptenophos
Roses, rhododendrons, other shrubs and fruits	Spray with gamma-HCH (BHC) or permethrin plus heptenophos

DISEASES

Fungal and bacterial diseases are possibly more of a problem in hedging than insect pests. Some of the very serious ones can actually kill the plants if action is not taken to control them.

The 'killer diseases' among those listed in the table are honey fungus, silver leaf and phytophthora root rot, while bacterial canker and canker can result in loss of branches. The most common of the diseases listed are black spot, leaf curl, mildew, honey fungus and rust.

With diseases such as black spot, leaf curl, mildew and rust it is best to carry out routine pre-ventative sprays before the diseases actually appear, as they are difficult to control once they establish themselves on plants.

The fungicides recommended must be used strictly according to the manufacturers' instructions. Spraying should be undertaken on a calm, preferably dull, day, but not during wet weather. They are best applied with a garden pressure sprayer, making sure you wet every part of the plant, including the undersides of leaves and shoot tips.

Right: *Victoria plum is one of many plants prone to rust.*

Name	Symptoms
Bacterial canker	Yellow leaves falling early, later other leaves with tiny round holes, bark splits, branches die
Black spot	Dark brown or blackish fringed spots on leaves. In a severe attack, leaves drop
Canker	Bark cracks and is killed; branches may die
Crown gall	Tumours develop on stems, and crowns at soil level
Honey fungus (*Armillaria mellea*)	Plants rapidly die. White fungal threads beneath bark. Honey coloured toadstools at base of stems or trunk
Leaf curl	Leaves become thickened, severely distorted and reddish in colour
Mildew	White powdery patches on leaves and shoot tips, both often becoming severely distorted
Phytophthora root rot	Roots are killed and foliage dies off from the base upwards. Eventually whole plant killed. Young plants are most vulnerable
Rust	Rust-coloured spots or pustules, generally on undersides of leaves
Silver leaf	Silvery sheen appears on leaves. Branches die; whole plant could die
Viruses	Various symptoms: stunted of distorted growth; leaves streaked, spotted or marbled with yellow

Plants attacked	Control
Cherries and plums	Spray with Bordeaux Mixture or liquid copper fungicide in late summer/autumn
Roses	Spray with thiophanate-methyl or propiconazole
Apples and pears	Cut out dead branches/shoots and/or bark; treat wounds with pruning compound
Trees, shrubs and fruits	Remove affected roots and stems if disfiguring
Wide range of trees and shrubs, as well as fruits and roses; especially privet	The use of proprietary control products containing phenols may save plants if used early. Dig up and burn dead plants and drench the holes with the control product; follow manufacturer's instructions for use
Peaches and almonds	Spray with Bordeaux Mixture or liquid copper fungicide twice in late winter and at autumn leaf-fall
Wide range of shrubs, plus roses and fruits	Spray with thiophanate-methyl or propiconazole
Conifers, heathers	Dig up and burn dying and dead plants. Do not replant in same piece of ground
Roses and many shrubs	Spray with liquid copper fungicide or propiconazole
Many fruits and some shrubs	Cut out and burn dead wood, between early and late summer
Many shrubs, trees and fruits	There is no cure. If plant severely affected dig it up and burn it. Keep aphids under control as they can spread viruses

CUTTINGS

If you want a lot of hedging plants and wish to save money, or if you want to replace an old hedge with a new one, consider raising your own plants from cuttings. A very wide range of hedging plants can be propagated very easily.

SEMI-RIPE CUTTINGS

These are prepared in late summer or autumn from current year's side shoots which are partially ripe or woody. The lower part of the shoots should be firm and brown, while the upper half should still be green and un-ripened. Prepare the shoots to a length of between 4 and 6in (100 and 150mm), by cutting the base immediately below a node (leaf joint), using a sharp knife. The leaves should be stripped from the lower one-third to half of each cutting. Then dip the lower ¼in (6mm) in hormone rooting powder to encourage rooting. Knock off the surplus on the side of the container.

The cuttings should be inserted up to the lower leaves in pots or seed trays of cutting compost—equal parts by volume of peat and course sand. Water them in and then if possible place in a warm situation to achieve quick rooting, such as an electrically heated propagating case in a greenhouse. A temperature of around 70°F (21°C) will ensure quick rooting. Alternatively place the containers of cuttings on staging in the greenhouse or in a cold frame outdoors. In lower temperatures rooting will take longer—perhaps up to six months for some subjects, particularly conifers.

When the cuttings have rooted they should be potted off into 3½in (90mm) pots of John Innes potting compost No. 1. If they were raised in heat they should be well hardened off in a cold frame prior to placing them in the open. When the young plants are well estab-lished in their pots they can be planted out—either into a nursery

Above: *Conifers can be propa-gated from semi-ripe cuttings, about 6in (150mm) long.*

bed to grow on, or direct in their final positions.

Plants which can be propagated from semi-ripe cuttings atriplex, berberis, buxus, ceanothus, chamaecyparis, cotoneaster, × cupressocyparis, elaeagnus, escallonia, euonymus, fuchsia, griselinia, hebe, hedera, hydrangea, ilex, jasminium, laurus, lavandula, lonicera (climbing), olearia, × osmarea, pittosporum, poncirus, potentilla, *Prunus cerasifera, P. cistena, P. lauro-cerasus, P. lusitanica, P. spinosa,* pyracantha, rhododendron, rosmarinus, santolina, senecio, syringa, taxus, thuja, tsuga, ulex and *Viburnum tinus.*

HARDWOOD CUTTINGS

Again current year's shoots are used but they are prepared when they are completely hard and woody, after the leaves have fallen, in the autumn or early winter. Using secateurs, cut the shoots into lengths of 6-8in (150-200mm), making the bottom cut just below a bud and the top cut immediately above a bud. Do not use the softer tips of shoots for cuttings. Leave all the buds intact and dip the lower ¼in (6mm) of each cutting into hormone rooting powder.

Cuttings are inserted to half to two-thirds of their length either in the open ground or in a cold frame

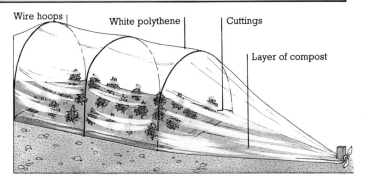

Wire hoops | White polythene | Cuttings

Layer of compost

Above: *Semi-ripe cuttings of conifers and shrubs can be rooted under low polythene tunnels.*

They are inserted in a bed of equal parts peat and coarse sand and take many months to form roots.

Above: *Many hedging shrubs can be propagated from hardwood cuttings up to 8in (200mm) long,*

taken in autumn/early winter. They are inserted deeply, either in the open ground or in a cold frame.

outdoors. Take out a V-shaped trench, stand the cuttings in it about 6in (150mm) apart, return the soil and firm in well. Most can be rooted in the open ground, but plants such as philadelphus, ribes, spiraea, symphoricarpos and wisteria will be better in a cold frame. The cuttings will be well rooted in a year, when they can be dug up and either planted in a nursery bed or direct into their final positions.

Plants which can be propagated from hardwood cuttings lingustrum, *Lonicera nitidia,* metasequoia (this needs to be rooted in pots in a propagator or heated greenhouse), philadelphus, populus, ribes, salix, spiraea, symphoricarpos, tamarix and wisteria. All of these root easily.

Above: *Rooted cuttings are best grown on in a nursery bed, until large enough for final planting.*

Many hedging and screening plants are easily raised from seeds, which are a very cheap means of obtaining large quantities of plants. Most subjects grow into sizeable specimens quickly, so it is by no means a slow process.

OBTAINING SEEDS

Several seed companies supply seeds of trees and shrubs suitable for hedging and screening. If, however you decide to collect your own, perhaps from trees and shrubs growing in your garden or in the gardens of friends, make sure you collect only from species of plants, not from hybrids or cultivars, for the seedlings from the latter will be very variable. Seedlings from species will be identical to their parents.

MAKING A SEED BED

Seeds of most trees and shrubs are sown outdoors during the spring. Choose an open, sunny, well-drained site for the seed bed and dig it to the depth of the spade, ideally in the previous autumn. If the ground is poorly drained throw the soil up into a raised bed about 3-4in (75-100mm)

high. A convenient width for a seed bed, whether raised or flat, is 3ft (900mm); it can, of course, be any length.

Final preparations just before sowing: break down the soil with a fork and firm it by treading systematically with the heels. Apply a general-purpose fertilizer at 4oz per square yard (113g per sq m) and rake it in, at the same time creating a level surface with about 1in (25mm) of fine loose soil in which to sow.

SOWING

Seeds of each subject can be sown in blocks across the bed. Take out shallow drills or furrows across the bed about 6in (150mm) apart, in which to sow the seeds. Use a draw hoe or pointed stick. Sow the seeds thinly and then cover with fine soil to a depth which equals approximately twice the diameter of the seeds. Alternatively, cover the entire seed bed with a ½in (12mm) layer of pea shingle.

It is essential to keep the soil moist during dry periods. Seeds of most subjects germinate quickly and by autumn the seedlings will be large enough to transplant to final site or nursery beds.

Above: *Seeds of most trees and shrubs can be sown outdoors in spring. Make a raised seed bed if the soil is poorly drained and sow the seeds in rows across the bed, spaced about 6in (150mm) apart. Make drills with a draw hoe.*

Above: *The drills should be quite shallow, and the seeds must be sown thinly. Cover them with fine soil to a depth which equals approximately twice their diameter. Alternatively cover the entire bed with pea shingle.*

Above: *Berries of pyracantha. These need a period of cold treatment before sowing, after which the seeds will germinate well.*

STRATIFICATION

Seeds of some subjects need a period of cold treatment (stratification) before sowing. These include cotoneaster, crataegus, ilex, pyracantha, rosa, sorbus and stranvaesia. In the autumn, mix the seeds with a quantity of moist sand, place in tins with drainage holes in the bottom, or in pots, and stand in a north-facing position in the garden, where they will be subjected to freezing during the winter. Protect them from mice. Then sow in the spring. There is no need to separate the seeds from the sand when sowing. If some do not germinate in the first spring, they may do so in the second spring from sowing.

SPECIAL CASES

Seeds of quercus (oaks) are best sown in the autumn, as soon as available. Those of rhododendron are very small and best sown in seed trays using an acid (lime-free) peat compost, or pure moist peat. They can be germinated in a greenhouse or cold frame, and the resultant seedlings pricked out (transplanted) into further seed trays to grow on.

BEST BETS

Plants which can be easily raised from seeds: carpinus, *Chamaecyparis lawsoniana,* cotoneaster, crataegus, *Cupressus macrocarpa*, fagus, hippophae, ilex, larix, metasequoia, picea, pinus, populus, quercus, pyracantha, *Rhododendron ponticum,* rosa, sorbus, stranvaesia and tilia.

OPEN-PLAN FRONT GARDEN

On some modern housing estates the front gardens are open-plan and tall hedges or walls are forbidden. Therefore you may have to consider other ideas for separating your garden from the public footpath.

LOW BOUNDARIES

Open-plan dwellers frequently take their lawns right up to the public footpath, but without any form of boundary passers-by tend to walk on the lawn edge, causing it to become worn and bare. One answer is to create a boundary with posts and ropes, or chains, or with low wire fencing, as described on pages 58-59.

Dwarf hedges are another idea, in the region of 12-18in (30-45cm) high. There are many suitable shrubs for this purpose, including the edging box, *Buxus sempervirens* 'Suffruticosa'. It is evergreen and grown as a formal hedge. *Berberis thunbergii* 'Atropurpurea Nana' is widely used, too. It is deciduous, with purple foliage, and should keep dogs out effectively, for it is prickly. Lavender, or *Lavandula angustifolia*, makes a good evergreen hedge in its dwarf forms, including 'Hidcote' and 'Munstead', both with lavender-blue flowers in summer. One of the cotton lavenders, *Santolina chamaecyparissus corsica* ('Nana'), forms a compact, dense, low hedge of evergreen silvery foliage.

HEATHER AND CONIFER BED

Instead of a low hedge you may prefer to lay out an irregularly shaped bed and plant it with heathers and dwarf conifers. Heathers are low-growing ground-cover shrubs and a collection of different varieties could provide colour almost all the year round. Dwarf conifers, which have attractive evergreen foliage, can be used as specimen plants in the heather bed, giving a contrast in height and a variation in shape and foliage texture.

● Some heathers must be grown in acid or lime-free soils, while others can be grown successfully in alkaline (limy or chalky) conditions.

● Both heathers and conifers need an open sunny position, the heathers especially being very intolerant of shade.

Below: *An open-plan front garden featuring dwarf conifers and heathers for all-year interest.*

● Both types are tough plants, so if those at the edge of the bed are occasionally trodden on, little damage will occur.

On alkaline soils Winter-flowering heathers are ideal for chalky soils, flowering not only all winter but well into spring. Choose *Erica carnea* (*E. herbacea*) varieties like 'Springwood Pink' (pink flowers); 'Springwood White' (white); 'Myretoun Ruby' (ruby red); and 'Foxhollow' (lavender, but with bright gold foliage all year round). There are many more besides these. Include, too, some varieties of winter-flowering *E.* × *darleyensis*, like 'Jack H. Brummage' (red-purple), 'Darley Dale' (pink); and 'Arthur Johnson' (rose-pink). Dwarf conifers to plant with these could include *Picea glauca* 'Albertiana Conica' with bright green foliage; *Thuja occidentalis* 'Rheingold' with deep gold foliage; the greyish or bluish green *Juniperus chinensis* 'Pyramidalis'; and the bright yellow *Chamaecyparis pisifera* 'Filifera Aurea'.

On acid soils With acid soil you can grow varieties of the summer-flowering heather or ling,

Below: *A hedge of edging box,* Buxus sempervirens *'Suffruticosa'. This is an evergreen shrub.*

Calluna vulgaris, like 'County Wicklow' (pink); and 'Robert Chapman' (purple flowers, but noted for its brilliant foliage: gold, bronze, red and yellow). Try also varieties of the summer-flowering *Erica cinerea*, such as 'Atrosanguinea Smith's Variety' (scarlet); *E. tetralix*, for example 'Alba Mollis' (white); *E. vagans*, like 'Mrs D. F. Maxwell' (deep rose-pink), and *Daboecia cantabrica*, for example 'Praegerae' (deep pink). Include, too, some winter-flowering heathers, more examples of which are *Erica* × *darleyensis* 'Silberschmelze' (white), and *E. herbacea* (*E. carnea*) 'Vivellii'. Dwarf conifers could include *Chamaecyparis pisifera* 'Boule-vard' (silvery blue foliage); *Picea glauca* 'Albertiana Conica' (bright green); and *Thuja occidentalis* 'Rheingold' (deep gold).

PROTECTING LAWN EDGES

If you decide to run the lawn right up to the public footpath, you could protect it with metal edging strips only a few inches high. Or you might lay pre-cast concrete edging stones with rounded tops, like mini kerb-stones. Heights vary from 6-10in (15-25cm). They are partially sunk in the ground and bedded in cement.

Another idea is to lay a strip of paving slabs or bricks along the lawn edge, which provides an attractive finish. The strip should be slightly below the level of the lawn so that you can mow over the lawn edge.

Alternatively, lay a row of perforated, pre-cast concrete lawn-reinforcement slabs around the edge of the lawn. The holes are filled with soil and sown with grass seed. You can mow over these slabs, provided they are level with the soil surface, and they provide a very durable surface, which can be trodden on frequently without ruining the grass.

MISCELLANEOUS BOUNDARIES

Although walls, fences and hedges are the obvious types of boundary, these by no means exhaust the possibilities of defining your garden. There are several simpler, less expensive ways, which can be just as attractive in the right setting.

POSTS AND ROPES

This type of boundary marker consists of short timber posts, about 12-18in (30-45cm) high, which support a single, thick, ornamental rope at the top. The rope is not tight but allowed to hang loosely in loops. Alternatively an ornamental steel or plastic chain may be used, perhaps painted black or white.

Posts and ropes do not really serve any practical purpose beyond that of a purely ornamental marker. They are most often used in open-plan front gardens, simply to remind neighbours or visitors not to tread on the lawn or flower beds. On an open-plan housing estate anything more conspicuous or substantial is usually banned.

Posts and ropes are reasonably cheap, pleasing in appearance and easy to erect. They are widely available from builder's merchants and from large hardware stores.

LOW WIRE FENCING

This serves the same sort of purpose as do posts and ropes. It is often sold in the UK as 'lawn edging', in heights of about 12in (30cm) and 24in (60cm), and is generally bought in rolls. It is generally made of plastic or PVC coated wire, often in green or white, in a range of different patterns.

This material is always easy to put up—just staple it onto stout timber posts of appropriate height. These may be painted to match the colour of the fencing.

Below: *Low posts and chains are often used to mark the boundaries of open-plan front gardens.*

SHRUB BORDERS

So far we have only considered the use of shrubs as formal and informal hedging. But perhaps you want an even more informal boundary. Why not consider growing shrubs naturally in a row where you want to mark your boundary or set up your screen?

Shrub borders can be suitable for both front- and back-garden boundaries. There is a wide choice of tall shrubs, well suited to the back garden, while dwarf ones might be specially suitable for front boundaries.

For the best effect plant a combination of evergreen and deciduous shrubs. A good balance is one-third evergreen and two-thirds deciduous.

● Shrubs for spring flowers: forsythia, ribes (flowering currant), kerria (Jew's mallow), chaenomeles (japonica), syringa (lilac), cytisus (broom) and genista (broom).

● Shrubs for summer flowers: philadelphus (mock orange), buddleia (butterfly bush), ceanothus, deutzia, hydrangea, weigela and viburnum.

● Shrubs for autumn interest: berberis, or barberries (berries); pyracantha, the fire-thorns (berries); rhus, the sumachs (coloured foliage), and *viburnum opulus,* the guelder rose (berries).

● Shrubs for winter interest: *Cornus alba* varieties, or dog-woods (coloured bark), *Daphne mezereum* (flowers), *Elaeagnus pungens* 'Maculata' (evergreen foliage), hamamelis, or witch hazels (flowers), and *Viburnum tinus*, or laurustinus (flowers, also evergreen foliage).

● Dwarf or low-growing shrubs: some of the berberis, caryopteris, dwarf cytisus, lavandula (lavenders), potentilla (shrubby cinquefoils), santolina (lavender cottons), senecios, and dwarf spiraeas.

Below: *A shrub border used as a boundary, including variegated cornus and a golden conifer.*

WALLS

Walls are alternatives to living boundaries such as hedges. But they needn't be dull or uninteresting, for with today's range of modern and traditional materials they can be features in themselves. One of their main advantages is that they need little maintenance.

PROS AND CONS

● Walls give a quicker effect than hedges.
● They are labour-saving, needing little maintenance.
● They are permanent (with hedges, there is a risk that some of the plants may die and create gaps).
● Walls are space-saving.
● You can build them to the exact height you wish.
● They can be made to blend in with the house.
● There are no problems with vandalism (as there can be with hedges).
● They can be used to support climbing plants.
On the debit side:
● High building cost is involved.
● Walls are time-consuming to build.
● They do not make good windbreaks (at least, solid walls do not).

WHERE TO USE WALLS

Walls are often used to define boundaries, especially at the front of the house. They can also be used within the garden, for dividing the plot, for screening and as ornamental features in their own right. They must, though, suit the style of the garden.

UTILITY WALLS

When a wall is built purely for functional purposes, its looks can still be improved by using the same bricks that were used for the house. If the house walls are rendered, the wall could be built of concrete building blocks and also rendered. Walls can even be painted with masonry paint (such as white or cream), to brighten up, say, a dingy backyard.

Bricks can be laid in various patterns, as shown in the drawings, perhaps in a combination of side on and end on. Flemish bond brickwork is particularly attractive.

Dwarf walls, up to 2ft (60cm) high, can be the thickness of a single brick. But walls over 2ft in height should be two bricks thick (even three for walls over, say, 6ft [1·8m] in height).

Above: *Combination of side-on and end-on bonding (left), and Flemish bond brickwork (right).*

Above: *Open brickwork walls (left) and a wall built of ornamental concrete walling blocks (right).*

ORNAMENTAL WALLS

Free-standing ornamental walls can also be used to define boundaries, or as features within the garden. Many manufacturers offer attractive ornamental concrete walling blocks.

For screening without considerably reducing light, why not try an open brickwork wall, as shown in the drawing? An alternative is screen-block walling, which consists of large, precast concrete blocks moulded in an openwork pattern. Perhaps these openwork walls are better suited to inside the garden, rather than as boundary walls—for example, to create a setting for a patio or to screen utility areas.

If you want a really fancy wall, consider a serpentine or curved brick wall.

SIZES OF WALLS

Generally the maximum height for boundaries, to give privacy, and for internal walls for screening, is 6ft (1·8m). If you want this height, or even higher walls, contact your local authority planning department and ask if there are any legal limits to the height of walls. For walls over 6ft (1·8m) high, and for very long walls, you should seek professional advice, as these may need special reinforcement, such as buttresses.

On the other hand there are many situations where lower walls, in the region of 3-4ft (1-1·2m), are more popular. Extra height may be created with fancy wrought-iron panels along the top.

DOUBLE WALLS FOR PLANTING

An attractive boundary for the front garden is a double wall, filled with soil for planting, and 3-4ft (1-1·2m) high. This could be constructed of bricks to match the house, ornamental concrete walling blocks, or natural stone to form dry-stone walls.

RETAINING WALLS

If you have a front garden which slopes down to the boundary you may need retaining walls to hold back the soil and perhaps to terrace the garden. Retaining walls must be strong—two or three bricks in thickness. Or you could use concrete building blocks, or natural stone to create dry-stone walls. Retaining walls must slope slightly in towards the bank of soil.

Above: *A serpentine wall (left), and a wall incorporating ornamental wrought-iron panels (right).*

Above: *A double wall for planting (left), and a dry-stone retaining wall for a sloping site (right).*

MATERIALS FOR WALLS AND FENCES

As with most commodities, one can pay as much or as little as one desires for walling and fencing materials. It all depends on quality. Here we take a look at what is available.

BRICKS

Generally, building walls with bricks entails higher cost and effort than, say, concrete walling blocks, and they're also more time-consuming to lay. However, there is no doubt that clay bricks look good in a garden as they are made of a natural material. It is often desirable to choose bricks to match the house, if possible. The standard size for bricks is 225 by 112·5 by 75mm.

CHOOSING BRICKS FOR GARDEN WALLS

Frost-resistant bricks (also known as special-quality bricks) are highly recommended. Moderately frost-resistant bricks (also known as ordinary-quality bricks) can be used for garden walls but advice should be sought from the manufacturer on suitability.

There are many brick types to choose from, but for an attractive finish, facing bricks (stocks) are often used. There are many colours and textures but they have only one or two attractive sides. Common bricks can be used where appearance is not vital. They are less costly, have no special facing and are therefore recommended where the wall is to be painted or rendered. Do not subject such walls to heavy stress or loads. Engineering bricks are dense, smooth and impervious to water—ideal for walls exposed to damp conditions or if part of the wall is to be below ground level.

Apart from clay bricks, frost-proof calcium silicate (sand lime or flint lime) bricks can also be used for free-standing garden walls. They come in a good range of strengths, and in a wide choice of colours and textures.

Above: *Aubrieta growing over a dry-stone wall.*
Below: *Brick pillars make attractive supports for front gates.*

CONCRETE WALLING BLOCKS

An alternative to bricks for building walls are ornamental concrete walling blocks and 'bricks' which come in various colours and textures. Some resemble natural stone. They are generally cheaper than bricks. Large blocks are quick, and easy, to lay. Plain utility building blocks (cheaper still) could be used if you want a painted or rendered wall. Some building blocks are light in weight and may not be suitable where great strength is needed.

Above: *Ranch-type fencing looks good in a modern setting.*
Below: *A combination of lapped fencing and trellis.*

Pierced or screen blocks are often cheaper than solid blocks and again quick to lay. They measure 12 by 12 by 4in (300 by 300 by 100mm); there are no half sizes and they cannot be cut. Various patterns are available.

NATURAL STONE

Expensive, but a delightful choice for garden walling. Stone is generally used only for low walls, about 3ft (1m) and below, whether dry-stone (laid without mortar) or bonded with mortar.

Ideally choose hard stone like granite or basalt. Various types of sandstone also look attractive, as does limestone. The best advice is to use local stone, as it is in keeping with the area and less costly to transport.

Stone comes in a mixture of sizes and is laid at random when building. One can also buy flattish stone, which can be built up in thin random layers to give a pleasing effect.

MATERIALS FOR FENCES

Close-boarded fencing A luxury type of fence, very long-lasting if built of hardwood; but softwood boards give good service if regularly painted or treated with wood preservative.

Lapped or interwoven fencing Generally made from larch or pine. Much cheaper than close-boarded, but it has a shorter life. Easily damaged if treated roughly.

Wattle and chestnut paling fencing Cheap forms of fencing with an expected life of 5-10 years. Wattle fencing is made from hazelwood.

Bamboo Although bamboo appears tough, the maximum life of a bamboo fence is around five years. It starts to look shabby after this.

Wire fencing Highly recommended are plastic or PVC coated products, or PVC mesh types, as they have a longer life than galvanized products, which eventually start to rust. Plastic-coated wire will, however, rust if the coating becomes damaged.

Trellis One cannot beat western red cedar trellis for longevity. Trellis in cheaper softwood is also available, but needs regular treatment with paint or wood preservative to ensure long service.

Ranch type, post and rail and paling fencing Generally constructed from softwoods, like pine. Be prepared to paint regularly to ensure a long life. Plastic ranch-style fencing is also available, but it attracts green algae.

BUILDING WALLS

Fairly brief but sufficient details are given here, for this is a big subject. However, further information can be obtained from *Creative Garden Projects* in this series.

PLANNING PERMISSION

This is needed if a wall along a boundary or highway used by vehicular traffic is to be more than 3ft 3in (1m) high; or 6ft 6in (2m) high within the garden. The wall must comply with local building regulations which govern safety aspects and construction.

FOUNDATION

Use trench foundation: a layer of rammed hardcore topped with concrete. Should be wider than the wall, the width equalling at least the depth of the concrete. The hardcore should be the same thickness as the concrete. A wall over six courses of bricks high needs a 20in (500mm) deep trench. Use levelling pegs to ensure perfectly level foundations. A suitable concrete mix is one part cement and five parts all-in aggregate.

FREE-STANDING BRICK OR BLOCK WALLS

The bricks or blocks are laid overlapping to provide a staggered bond for rigidity. Simplest is the stretcher bond (for single-thickness walls), the bricks being butted end to end and overlapping by half on alternate courses.

More complex (for double-thickness walls): courses of stretchers (bricks laid end to end), alternated with courses of headers (bricks laid across the width of the wall). Walling blocks can be laid in the same way.

Garden walls are best provided with a brick damp-proof course: two courses of low water absorption bricks at the base of the wall. Very long walls will need the support of piers or buttresses about 12ft (3·6m) apart.

Build up the wall at either end first, and then fill in the middle—bricks can if necessary be cut here. A good tip is to dry lay about four courses of bricks to acquire the knack of bonding them. A mortar mix for bricklaying consists of one part cement and six parts builders' sand.

Use taut strings to keep the courses straight when laying, and a spirit level to check vertical alignment at every course.

Shape the mortar joints once the mortar has stiffened: press it into a V-shape with the edge of the trowel.

Cap the wall with coping (specially shaped bricks or blocks) to deflect the rain: for example, half-rounded or bevel-edged

Below left: *Walls need to be built on a trench foundation.*
Below right: *Build up the wall at each end first and then fill in the middle (where bricks can be cut).*

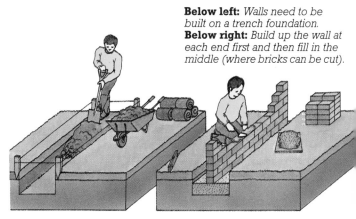

bricks. Flat or bevelled coping stones (wider than wall) are also available, together with capping stones to top piers. Ideally provide a damp-proof course immediately below the coping. This arrangement will prevent the wall from becoming damp.

SCREEN-BLOCK WALLS

Blocks are laid in stack bond, one on top of the other. They are supported with piers about 6-10ft (1·8-3m) apart. These are formed from hollow cubes called pilasters which have slots to take the blocks. The piers are supported through the centre with metal reinforcing rods embedded in the foundations. The pilasters are filled with concrete as building proceeds.

Use foundations as described above, and finish off with bevelled coping and pilaster cappings.

DOUBLE WALLS

An ornamental feature for planting, usually 3-4ft (1-1·2m) high. Build on double trench foundations (constructed as described above) and insert metal ties at intervals across the two walls for rigidity. Use frost-resistant bricks. Fill double walls with light to medium topsoil or John Innes potting compost No. 2. The latter is more expensive than topsoil.

Below left: *Use taut strings to keep all the courses level when laying, and a spirit level to check horizontal and vertical alignment at every course.*

RETAINING WALLS

As these retain soil, say on a bank or sloping site, they are subjected to considerable pressure so need to be constructed with a double or treble thickness of bricks or blocks. Drainage holes must be left at intervals along the base of the wall. Do not build any higher than 4ft (1·2m) without guidance from your local authority.

Drystone retaining walls are particularly attractive and highly recommended. Give them a slight backward slope into the bank—in fact, they should only tilt back on the outer face—a slope of about 2in in 12in (50mm in 300mm) being adequate. The wall should be wedge shaped.

Excavate the bank to form a vertical terrace and build the wall hard against this. For a small wall build on a rubble-filled trench 24in (600mm) deep and twice as wide as the top of the wall. Large walls need hardcore and concrete foundations.

The stones are laid at random, endeavouring to interlock them for strength. At intervals lay large wide stones across the wall and into the bank to act as ties. As building proceeds add soil between the joints for plants.

Make sure the soil is packed firmly behind the wall as it is being built. Top the completed wall with large flat stones to act as coping.

Below right: *Shape the mortar joints once the mortar has stiffened: press it into a V-shape with the edge of the trowel (weatherstruck type of pointing).*

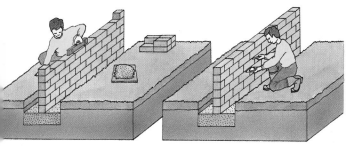

CLEANING AND REPAIRING WALLS

After a time, walls can become dirty and green growth may build up on them, which is unsightly. Weather also takes its toll on walls and so repairs may be needed. Do not neglect brickwork for if moisture and frost start to penetrate a wall, it can deteriorate more quickly than most people imagine.

ALGAE AND MOSS

The green film or slime which sometimes appears on walls is formed by algae, which are primitive plants. Moss may also grow, forming mats or hummocks of growth. Both are liable to establish on walls in damp conditions, or if the air circulation around a wall is poor.

Algae and moss will not harm the wall but they render it unsightly, particularly so with painted or rendered walls.

Treat walls with a commercial algicide (as used in the building trade), which will kill off algae and moss. It is particularly important to uses an algicide if you intend painting the wall. If not treated, the paint could eventually flake off. Apply the algicide according to the manufacturer's instructions, and keep it away from plants.

If the wall is not to be painted you could use a horticultural algicide and moss killer, of the concentrated tar-oil emulsion type, containing phenols. It can be applied with a garden pressure sprayer, using a coarse spray, but do not let it come into contact with cultivated plants. Apply according to the maker's instructions. Once the algae and moss are dead the wall can be cleaned by scrubbing, using detergent in the water.

MASONRY PAINTS

If you want to paint a garden wall do not use emulsion paint, as some people do, for this has a short life outdoors. Instead, use exterior masonry paints. The cement-based types are very long-lasting, as are those that contain fine sand.

Masonry paints come in many colours but for garden walls the various shades of white and cream, and perhaps grey, are recommended.

Application can be by brush—say a 6in (15cm) wide brush—or suitable paint roller. Masonry paint can be applied direct to the brickwork, concrete or cement rendering. If an existing painted surface is still in good condition mimimum preparation will be needed. However, if it is flaking the loose material should be stripped off and the entire surface treated with stabilizing solution. Use this solution, too, if the surface is very absorbent or dusty.

REPOINTING BRICKWORK

The mortar bonding between bricks may start to crumble and fall out after a period of time, the length of time depending on the age of the wall and local climatic conditions. This must be replaced or the wall will quickly deteriorate, as frost and moisture will penetrate.

Chisel out the old crumbling

Above left: *Before painting a wall with masonry paint moss and algae must be scraped off.*
Above: *Then the wall should be treated with a commercial algicide, working it well in with a stiff brush. This will kill off any remaining moss and algae. If you do not use an algicide the paint could eventually flake off, and ruin the effect.*

Above: *Paint with a hammered enamel finish gives wrought iron-work a very smart appearance. Only one thick coat is needed.*

mortar to a depth of ½in (12mm) or so and refill, using a builders' trowel. A suitable mortar mix for repointing consists of one part cement and six parts builders' sand.

The pointing must deflect rainwater, so press the mortar into a V-shape, known as weatherstruck pointing.

Do not forget to check coping on top of the wall and repoint this if necessary—or replace if it has badly deteriorated. Faulty coping will allow moisture to penetrate.

WROUGHT IRONWORK

If you have any wrought-iron panels on walls, iron railings, gates, etc, keep these painted to prevent rust setting in. Ordinary gloss paint, preceded by an undercoat, can be used, or you may prefer a paint with a hammered enamel finish. Only one thick coat of this is needed, even if the surface is rusty. Not much preparation of rusty surfaces is required. Just rub off the loose rust with a wire brush. No primer need be applied; indeed this paint stops rust. You should find hammered enamel paint in good DIY shops.

FENCES

The quickest way to form a boundary, or to provide screening, is to put up fences. However, fencing needs to be chosen with care for it should suit the style of garden and house. Fortunately there are many kinds of fencing to choose from.

SOLID FENCES

A solid fence will be needed for complete privacy and screening, for example up to 6ft (1·8m) in height. Unlike hedges, solid fences are not good windbreaks—they do not filter the wind but cause turbulence on the leeward side, especially in exposed or windy sites. If, however, this problem does not arise, solid fences have the advantage of being good supports for climbing plants.

Close-boarded timber Constructed on site, this makes a rigid, durable structure, though not cheap. The fence is constructed from vertical or horizontal boards, the former fixed to horizontal rails supported by posts, and the latter directly to the posts.

Prefabricated fencing Often made of lapped (i.e. overlapping) or interwoven strips of larch, this type of panel fencing is very popular, and panels can be purchased in a range of convenient sizes. They are a comparatively cheap form of solid fencing. Both close-boarded and prefabricated fences are frequently used in suburban gardens, for example as boundaries between back gardens. They seem to go with all styles of architecture, since timber, being a natural product, rarely looks out of place in any garden.

Wattle Available in ready-made panels, wattle is a close weave of hazelwood, which looks particularly good in country gardens. Wattle can be used as a boundary fence, but is more often used as a cheap screen—for example, to hide utility parts of the garden.

Bamboo Ready-made bamboo screens are also used for screening small areas and look particularly attractive in a simple modern setting.

Concrete This type consists of concrete panels slotted into channels in the concrete supporting posts. Plain concrete is hardly attractive for garden use, but panels with an ornamental finish would not look out of place in, say, an ultra-modern setting. Used mainly as a back-garden boundary, and enhanced by training climbers up it.

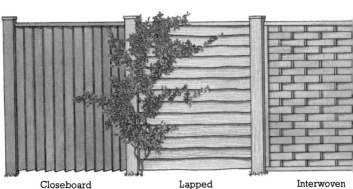

Closeboard   Lapped   Interwoven

Above: *From left to right: close boarded timber fencing is built on site; lapped panel fencing is popular and comparatively cheap, as are interwoven fencing panels (often made of larch).*

OPENWORK FENCES

As they filter the wind, openwork fences make better windbreaks than solid ones. They do not create a 'closed-in' feeling and this may be important in small pocket-handkerchief gardens. Some are very inconspicuous—particularly important if you do not want to hide an attractive view.

Mesh fencing Generally sold in rolls, mesh fencing can be galvanized or plastic-coated wire netting; galvanized or plastic-coated chain-link (more durable than wire netting); or proprietary plastic mesh. All are compara-tively cheap and easy to erect. Mesh fencing is often used for back-garden boundaries, especially on modern housing estates, and it always keeps out dogs and other pets. Heights up to 6ft (1·8m) are available and you have perfect supports for climbing plants.

Trellis Timber trellis panels are often used for screening/division within the garden; again ideal supports for climbers. They look good both in town and country gardens. The panels come in a range of sizes, with square or diamond pattern. There are some companies in the UK who specialize in fancy trellis panels with shaped tops.

Paling or picket fencing Usually 3-4ft (1-1·2m) high, this consists of narrow vertical boards (rounded or pointed at the top) spaced about 3in (7·5cm) apart. An ideal choice for a country garden, being particularly suitable for a front boundary. It is not too expensive and comes in kit form. Paint it white, or treat with garden timber preservative in natural colours.

Split chestnut palings Consists of split vertical chestnut stakes linked top and bottom by galvanized wire, supplied in rolls, with heights of 3-6ft (1-2m). Comparatively cheap and easy to put up, it is often used as a temporary fence until a boundary hedge becomes established.

Ranch type Horizontal bars of timber or PVC, with spaces between. Make your own or buy a kit. Looks especially good as a boundary for gardens on modern housing estates, especially in combination with an open-plan front garden. Generally painted white.

Post and rail This has less bars than ranch-type fencing and is very much a country-garden fence. Ideal for surrounding paddocks. Looks good whether painted white or treated with a wood-coloured horticultural timber preservative.

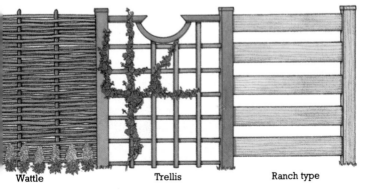

Wattle   Trellis   Ranch type

Above: *From left to right: wattle fencing looks particularly good in country gardens; trellis panels* *come in various designs; and ranch-type fencing, in timber or plastic, is suitable for modern gardens.*

GATES

Gates should always be chosen to suit the style of the house together with the style of the fences, hedges or walls that surround it. All too often, little or no thought is put into choosing a gate and as a result many look ridiculously out of place. A smart, well-chosen gate that is kept in good condition does a lot to enhance a property, while a poor or badly neglected one has the opposite effect.

THE RIGHT HEIGHT

Gates are generally incorporated into a boundary wall, fence or hedge. If possible try to make the gate the same height as the boundary as it will look more impressive. In other words, try not have a 3ft (1m) high gate in a 6ft (1·8m) high wall or fence; although it must be said that this is often seen. Obviously if you have a tall boundary and decide to invest in high gates, the cost will be very much higher. Many front boundaries, however, are fairly low, perhaps 3-4ft (1-1·2m) in height; there are plenty of gates available to match these heights, both singles and doubles.

ENSURING A VIEW

If you have a tall, solid boundary, such as a wall, fence or thick hedge, it might be a good idea to have an openwork gate to give you a view of the outside world, especially if it is a particularly pleasing view. You will thus be offering passers-by a tantalizing glimpse of your garden, so you will have to decide whether or not you want this.

Wrought-iron gates, both singles and doubles, are of the openwork type and come in a very wide range of patterns, from simple to ornate designs. Wrought iron always looks good with brickwork, simulated or natural stone, and hedges,

Above: *Wrought-iron gates are best painted either black or white, and can be relied on to look good in any setting.*

Above: *A solid timber gate set in a high boundary wall, guaranteed to give complete privacy.*
Right: *An attractive boundary—wrought-iron gates and a mixed shrub border featuring forsythia and ornamental cherry.*

whether formal or informal. Tall wrought-iron gates often come with an attractive rounded top, so the opening is in the form of an archway.

One sees wrought-iron gates painted in various colours, but there is nothing to beat black for a really smart appearance, using gloss or matt-finish paint. In certain situations, though, white wrought-iron gates may be more appropriate, especially in a very modern setting.

GATES TO MATCH FENCING

Of course, you may prefer to match the gate with fencing. For a solid timber fence you may be able to obtain a gate in close-boarded timber. You can also buy lapped or interwoven timber gates to match fencing panels.

If you are a DIY enthusiast you may be able to adapt a lapped or interwoven fencing panel into a gate: generally this works out cheaper than buying a ready-made gate.

Paling and ranch-type gates can be made or bought for these styles of fencing. Double ranch-type gates are often used at the entrances to driveways.

GATEPOSTS

Gates are only as good as the posts that support them. In low brick or stone walls, such as front-boundary walls, gates can be supported by brick or stone pillars which are built with the wall. Wrought-iron gates, though, are often supplied with metal posts if needed, for instance if you are putting up a gate in a hedge.

Timber gates are generally hung from timber posts, of the type that support the fence.

ERECTING FENCES AND GATES

As with walls, fences and gates are treated fairly briefly as comprehensive details are to be found in *Creative Garden Projects*. Nevertheless the basic details are here, sufficient to enable you to erect these features. Don't forget about planning permission: details as for walls.

POSTS

Timber posts, at least 3 by 3in (75 by 75mm) are often used for fences. You should first treat them with wood preservative; as well as painting it onto the wood, you should soak the ends of the posts overnight in a preservative. Use a wooden cap at the top of each post. Spacing of posts for fencing is usually 6ft (2m) apart.

If you wish to concrete posts into the ground, take out holes 24in (600mm) deep for fences over 4ft (1·2m) high, or 18in (450mm) for shorter ones. Add 6in (150mm) to these depths to allow for a layer of rammed hardcore for drainage. Set the post in the hole, wedge it upright (check with spirit level), and fill in with a fairly dry concrete mix—one part cement, four parts all-in aggregate.

Much easier to use are metal post supports, which consist of a steel spike, on top of which is a square 'cup' into which the post is slotted. The post support is first hammered into the ground, until the base of the cup is level with the soil.

TIMBER FENCES

Panel fencing To erect this type of fencing, insert the first post, then secure a panel to it with 3in (75mm) galvanized nails. Then insert the next post. The panels are held *between* the posts.
Close-boarded fencing When putting up close-boarded fencing the horizontal rails (arris rails) between posts are put in as the posts are inserted—they are mortised into the posts. Two or three rails are usually needed.

Then horizontal gravel boards—6in by 1in (150mm by 25mm) timber—are nailed to cleats at the base of the posts. The feather-edged boards rest on the top edge of the gravel boards, and are nailed to the arris rails.

The boards should overlap by about ½in (12mm), the thick edge overlapping the thin edge. If horizontal boards are desired, nail these direct to the posts. Finally a bevelled coping strip should be nailed along the top of the fence.

FENCES IN OTHER MATERIALS

Chain-link and wire mesh
These and similar fences are often supported by galvanized steel posts concreted into the ground. The end posts should have diagonal struts. The posts support two or three horizontal heavy-duty galvanized wires, which should be really tight, achieved with straining bolts in the end posts. The wires pass through holes in the intermediate posts. Attach the fencing material to the wires with tying wire.
Ranch-type and post and rail fences Simply constructed with timber posts, the horizontal bars being nailed direct to them.

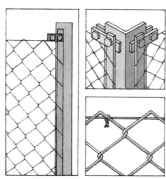

Above: *Chain-link fencing can be supported with metal or concrete posts and strained horizontal galvanized wires. Tension is easily obtained with the aid of straining bolts in the end posts.*

Above: *When hanging a gate, wedge it in place with scraps of timber. Check with a spirit level to ensure it's completely level. This gate has substantial T-hinges.*

Split chestnut palings The roll of ready-made fencing is stapled to wooden posts or chestnut poles, the end ones being at least 3in (75mm) diameter, and braced with diagonal struts.

Paling Use timber posts and two horizontal rails. Nail vertical boards to rails, using galvanized nails. Space 3in (75mm) apart.

Trellis Erected in the same way as panel fencing (above).

Wattle The panels are nailed directly to timber posts.

TYPES OF GATE SUPPORT

There are various supports for gates. Brick or stone piers, for instance, which can incorporate projecting hinge pins on which

to hang the gates. The pins are inserted when building the piers. Use bolt-on double-strap hinges on wooden gates, which drop over the hinge pins.

Gates can also be hung on timber posts, 4in (100mm) square, planed smooth, with bevelled or rounded tops to shed rainwater, and treated with timber preservative. To set the posts the right distance apart lay them on the ground with the gate between them. Allow a gap of ¼in (6mm) between the gate stiles (the vertical sections at each side) and the posts. Then cut a length of timber to fit exactly between the posts and use this as a guide when inserting them.

PUTTING UP THE POSTS

Posts should extend at least 18in (450mm) below ground. Set them on a base of rammed hardcore, about 4in (100mm) thick. When you are hanging the gate ensure there is clearance of 2in (50mm) beneath it.

When the posts are inserted in the prepared holes, pack some hardcore around them and set them vertically, using a spirit level. Ensure the tops are level, using a straight-edge board and spirit level. Support the posts with temporary struts and then fill the holes to the top with concrete.

HANGING THE GATE

To hang the gate, stand it between the posts on scraps of timber. Then pack each side with timber to hold the gate firm. Use a spirit level at the top of the gate to ensure it is level. If you are using T-hinges, hold them against the gate and post and mark the screw holes. If you are using strap-type hinges, these are fixed to the gate first. Then the gate is set in place as above, but in the open position, and the screw holes are marked on the post for the hooks. Then screw the hooks in place and finally hang the gate.

TIMBER PRESERVATION AND REPAIRS

Timber soon deteriorates if not regularly treated with preservative or paint. Once moisture is able to penetrate, rot quickly sets in and spreads. So be prepared to treat timber every two to three years, depending on local climate and weather conditions.

TIMBER PRESERVATIVES

It is essential to use horticultural timber preservative if plants are being grown on the fence, trellis or whatever, as it will not harm them. Avoid preservatives which give off harmful fumes, such as creosote; these are used only if there are no plants in the vicinity. Remember they can still give off fumes several years after application, particularly during hot weather.

Use a good, modern horticultural wood preservative, such as the type which has the active ingredient furmecyclox (an organic

Below: *Fencing panels are often pre-treated with preservative.*
Below right: *Timber fences must be treated regularly to stop rot.*

fungicide). This is non-fading and as it is water-based, brushes and splashes are easily cleaned with plain water. Various colours are available: red cedar, dark oak and golden chestnut. As regards preparation of the timber, first brush off any algae, moss or grime with a stiff brush. Then apply the preservative by brush, when the wood is dry—and the weather also. Treat both sides of the fence if possible.

PAINTS

Some features you may want to paint rather than use a timber preservative—such as gates, ranch-type fencing and picket fencing.

For raw timber, first apply a priming paint, then an undercoat and finally the finishing coat, using gloss paint suitable for exterior use.

Old paintwork should be treated as follows: first rub it down well with glasspaper (or use an electric sander to speed up the job). Only a light rubbing down is necessary if the paint is still in good condition. However, make sure you remove any green algae and

grime. Any flaking paint should certainly be removed, and if you get down to the bare wood retouch with priming paint. Apply an undercoat followed by the finishing coat.

Apply paint only when the timber is completely dry. To keep paintwork in tip-top condition, and to maintain a good appearance, paint fences and gates every three years.

MICROPOROUS PAINT

You may be interested in trying microporous paint, which is fairly new on the market. The film of paint has tiny pores in it which allow any moisture in the wood to escape as vapour. Moisture is not, therefore, trapped behind the coat of paint, as it can be with ordinary paints. Trapped moisture allows rot to set in and causes the paint to blister, crack or peel. This does not happen with microporous paint. It is applied to bare wood,

Below: *Use a horticultural wood preservative, as this will not damage plants which are near to or growing on the fence.*

neither primer nor undercoat being used, though the manufacturers do recommend that you use a wood preservative first. Many colours are available, including white, which is a popular choice for garden work.

REPAIRS TO OLD FENCES

Some types of fences are not easily repaired and are therefore best replaced if damaged or past their useful life, for example the lapped and interwoven panels. Close-boarded, ranch-type, paling fencing and the like can be repaired by the handyman. It is often an easy task to put in new pieces of timber.

Fencing posts, however, are often the first to go, decaying at ground level. These days it is possible to re-use posts which have rotted at the base by cutting away the bases and inserting them in metal post supports, which are driven into the ground. First, though, treat the posts (paying particular attention to the bases) with wood preservative. Bases of posts should be soaked in preservative for several hours.

INDEX

PICTURE CREDITS

Artists
Copyright of the artwork illustration on the pages following the artists' names is the property of Salamander Books Ltd.
Dee McLean (Linden Artists): 11, 22-23, 34, 35, 38-39, 40-41, 47, 52, 53, 54, 60-61, 64-65, 72, 73

Photographers
The publishers wish to thank the following photographers and companies who have supplied photographs for this book. The photographs have been credited by page number, and position on the page where appropriate: B (Bottom), T (Top), BL (Bottom Left) etc.
Eric Crichton: 4-5, 6, 8, 9, 10, 12, 13, 16, 17 (L), 17 (R), 28, 29, 32-33, 37, 40, 42 (T), 42 (B), 43, 45, 46 (T), 46 (B), 53, 5, 56, 57, 58, 59, 62 (T), 62 (B), 63 (T), 63 (B), 66, 67 (T), 70 (T), 70 (B), 71, 74 (L), 74 (R)
Neil Holmes: Endpapers
Hunting Specialised Products Ltd: 67 (B)
Merrist Wood Agricultural College for photographic facilities.
Alan Toogood: 44
Michael Warren: 22, 36, 49, 51